10 THOUGHTS TO PONDER

10 THOUGHTS TO PONDER

Book 3

FRANK BALL

10 Thoughts to Ponder — Book 3
A Buffet for the Inquisitive Mind
By Frank Ball

Copyright © 2026. All rights reserved.

No part of this publication may be reproduced, stored in a retrieval system, or transmitted—electronic, mechanical, photocopy, recording, or any other way—without the written prior permission of the copyright holder, except as provided by US copyright law.

Scripture quotations are from *The Discussion Bible* (TDB) © 2008, 2018, 2019, 2020, 2023 by Frank Ball. All rights reserved.

First Printing

Roaring Lambs Publishing
17110 Dallas Pkwy Ste 260
Dallas, TX 75248

Phone: 972.380.0123
Email: info@RoaringLambs.org
FBall@RoaringLambs.org

RoaringLambs.org
FrankBall.org

Introduction

People sometimes ask where I get so many interesting thoughts. If you think God might be my source, then give him credit—not me. But please don't blame him for my off-the-wall comments or foolish ideas. I'll gladly take responsibility for those.

On the other hand, I've often found that even my wrong perceptions can open the door to a clearer grasp of what's true. A thought that first feels out-of-focus may sharpen my vision of reality. So perhaps any of the ten random thoughts on this page can spark your faith, draw you nearer to God, and enrich your personal stories of his greatness.

This *10 Thoughts to Ponder* book series grew out of more than thirty years of asking questions, exploring possibilities, and recording daily insights. They help me remember, reinforce truth, and grow in God's knowledge and wisdom.

One day when picking up my grandson from high school, I asked, "What did you learn today?" His quick reply was typical: "Nothing." I wasn't about to let that slide. "Really? After sitting through all your classes and hearing everything your teachers had to say, you didn't learn a single thing?" With a little more prodding, he finally came up with an answer—which I knew he could. From then on, as soon as he opened the car door, his greeting became: "Grampa, did you know …?" And from there, our rides were always filled with lively, thought-provoking conversations.

Later, I imagined God asking me, "What did you learn today?" I heard myself answering, "Nothing." I knew what his reply would be: "Really? After everything I've done in your life today, you didn't learn a single thing?" That realization nudged me toward a more disciplined habit of writing down new thoughts as soon as they crossed my mind—so they could be remembered and shared. And if God should ask, I would have something to say.

I'm delighted to share whatever thoughts might encourage you and help you flourish in this crazy, mixed-up world. Life can be confusing, and sometimes a single word, phrase, or story is all it takes to bring clarity, hope, and a better sense of direction.

If something resonates in your heart, my prayer is that it isn't simply my idea, but the Lord himself whisper his truth to you. Should that happen, give him all the praise. He's the true source of wisdom. As for me, I'll gladly settle for honorable mention, grateful to be used as one of his messengers.

— Frank Ball

Gift of Giving

When I was little, I got fifty cents to buy Christmas presents for my brother and sister. In those days, you could buy an ice cream cone or a big candy bar for a nickel, so it was easy enough to find something of value at the dime store. The challenge was how to get the greatest value for just a quarter and have it be something they would really appreciate. That took a lot of shopping.

I learned that giving was even more fun than getting.

> *The measure you give will be the measure you get.*
> *— Mark 4:24*

Ten Thoughts to Ponder

1. A dull mind needs external abrasion because it cannot easily sharpen itself.
2. Two things are "married" when they are inseparably joined, which is who we should be with God in Christ Jesus.
3. Today is the most important part of the process that can take us to where God wants us to be.
4. If people can't anticipate God's miraculous work in their lives, then their expectations cannot be very good.
5. Satan's fatal mistake was believing he could be God, not satisfied with being *like* God.
6. God cannot change who we have been, but if we will accept his forgiveness and surrender to his desire, he will change who we are and who we will be.
7. When we surrender our imperfections to the Lord, he can work perfectly in our lives.
8. Confidence in our future with God is good, but confidence in the present that leads to that future is even better.
9. Great marketing will sell some really great lies and some very bad books.
10. If we worship a god of our own making, we can feel good about ourselves because we're in control.

Questions for Further Thought

- What is the best criteria for giving?
- How should we respond to people who ask for money?

Tough Times

One of the great challenges we face in understanding the Christmas story is realizing that Mary, Joseph, and others didn't know what we know about their futures.

They faced difficult times and had to trust God every step of the way, just like we do. Why? Because they didn't know.

> *Enemies may attack us, but God stands with us. We may be knocked to the ground, but God will raise us up.*
> *— 2 Corinthians 4:9*

Ten Thoughts to Ponder

1. To see a miracle, we need only to recognize God's hand at work.
2. Jesus expressed God's intention, that we are gods, but we are foolish to think that we are in control, since we are not God.
3. Really difficult work appears to be easy—to those who have never done such work.
4. In following the Lord, we shouldn't drag our feet, but we shouldn't be in too big a hurry, either.
5. If life were easy, it would be worthless.
6. To be in the center of God's will, we surrender our desires and acquire God as our peacemaker and pacemaker.
7. One of my great strengths is not knowing what I'm doing and knowing that I don't know.
8. God's promise for transformation, changing us from one glory to a greater glory, is hindered by our satisfaction in being who we are.
9. Future opportunities are of little value unless they help me with what is needed today.
10. Everybody on Earth experiences good and evil, but people don't always recognize the distinction, allowing evil to look good to them.

Questions for Further Thought

- Why might trusting God be difficult in troublesome times?
- What proof do we have that God's promises will be fulfilled?

Birth Announcement

Our birth announcements can give only the names of the baby, parents, and grandparents. It can list the height and weight at the beginning, but only God knows what the child will accomplish in life.

At the birth of our Savior, the Lamb of God to be sacrificed for our sins, the shepherds heard who Jesus was born to be.

My good news will bring great joy to everyone. Today in the city of David, a savior has been born, the anointed Messiah.
— *Luke 2:10–11*

Ten Thoughts to Ponder
1. To be appreciated, we must give of ourselves.
2. We should be desperate for God's transformation to do what we could never do on our own.
3. Perfection is a figment of our imagination—unless God has done the work.
4. Our passionate aggression to believe harder and get what we want can be effective only when it is begging for God to give us what he wants.
5. If we accept who we are in Christ, we have no need to be ashamed.
6. The most wonderful feeling of God's presence comes from knowing we are in the center of doing God's perfect will.
7. Our greatest pleasures are to enjoy to the fullest whatever pleases the Lord.
8. I need to know whatever I need to know, but if I don't know what I need to know, I need to pray a lot.
9. Mountain-moving depends upon God's power and my cooperation.
10. When we recognize our need and turn to God, we are smarter than Artificial Intelligence can ever be, because he alone has the correct answers.

Questions for Further Thought
- Why do some people think they can know what only God knows?
- How can parents be the best help to their children?

Puzzled

Dad walked into his blind son's bedroom and saw his missing pocket watch lying in pieces on the dresser. Evidently, his curious son had wanted to discover what made it tick.

Johnny couldn't see how Daddy knew how the pieces got there.

The puzzle was solved when Dad said, "You're blind, son, and I am not."

We should be thankful that God sees so much more than we do.

> *The Lord says, "I don't think the way you think, and my methods are different from yours. As the stars are so distant from Earth, so are my thoughts and methods far above yours.*
> *— Isaiah 55:8–9*

Ten Thoughts to Ponder

1. Faith is how we get ourselves out of the way so God can have his way.
2. I need God's direction toward what he knows is most needed, because there's no way I can figure it out and know for sure that I have figured it out.
3. An incorrect guess is not as good as not guessing at all.
4. I have no desire to forget my mess-ups, because I need them to reveal the greatness of God's miracle in my life.
5. Your greatest of rewards is to find a treasure you have lost.
6. Confidence in God's promise is good—if we really know what it is, and we know what we need to do to see it fulfilled.
7. Success that is easy is called luck.
8. Thinking I can do all things is foolishness—unless I know the One who is the only One who can make that possible.
9. If words contain no reward, people have no reason to read.
10. What God wants to accomplish cannot be accomplished until he has accomplished what he wants to accomplish now.

Questions for Further Thought

- What steps can we take that will help us see what God sees?
- How might asking lots of questions be helpful, even when we can't find an answer.

Can'tAthalon

A neighbor boy and I tied a handlebar rope swing in the tree in his front yard. Taking turns, we swung out from the porch and leaped as far across the lawn as we could. Week after week, we moved a wooden stake to mark our best-ever record. One day, I must have done everything just right, because I flew two feet beyond our best mark.

We never used that rope swing again. Why? Because neither of us believed we could ever do any better.

Never tire of doing good, for a harvest of blessing is certain if you never give up on God.
— Galatians 6:9

Ten Thoughts to Ponder
1. Being out of control is nothing like the pleasure of being under God's control.
2. Intrigue would be meaningless if there were no opportunity for discovery and increased value.
3. When engaged in a business for profit, our top priority should be to help others, and then we'll have less reason to worry.
4. Creativity must first be aware of what is. After that, we can see what isn't but could be.
5. Some people live in a dreamlike, fantasy world, but reality is much more exciting and unbelievable.
6. The only way to avoid mistakes is not doing anything, and that's a mistake.
7. I don't need to know anything until I need to know it … and only God knows what and when that will be.
8. When I am caught up in trivial but urgent demands, I can easily ignore what is most important.
9. We should always hunger for more of God and doing his will, because he is the greatest of all treasures.
10. Some of our most powerful stories are not yet completed.

Questions for Further Thought
- Why might it be dangerous to think we can do something when actually, we can't?
- How can we know when to quit and when to keep going?

Value of Cheating

While my dad was out of the room, I moved a chess piece just one square over to give me a stronger position. At the time, he didn't say anything. I'm not positive, but I'm pretty sure he let me win.

Afterward, he said, "You didn't win. You might fool others, but you can't fool yourself. You know you cheated. God knows you cheated. So the two most important people in the universe know you didn't win. You lost, because cheating makes it impossible to win."

Never lie, cheat, or steal. The Lord detests lying, but he loves people whose words can be trusted.
— Leviticus 19:11; Proverbs 12:22

Ten Thoughts to Ponder
1. The peace of God defies all understanding because it thrives in the midst of the storm.
2. I don't have to understand what God needs me to do, but I do need to do whatever God knows I need to do.
3. As much as living requires breathing in and out, God's gifts require both receiving and giving.
4. Today, I cannot do what must be done tomorrow, but I can wind up doing tomorrow what I really needed to do today.
5. Like a diamond, we have our greatest value when shaped to perfectly radiate God's light.
6. Perseverance sets no limits but is relentless in its effort.
7. I can be content being blind, as long as I can feel Jesus holding my hand, guiding me.
8. If God will help me with each step, I will learn to walk, run, and leap as I praise him in all things.
9. When truth is received, it must replace a misconception.
10. If we know the truth that sets us free, we should be as aware of God's presence as much as the air we breathe.

Questions for Further Thought
- What are the greatest motivators to lie, cheat, and steal?
- Why might people expect their own elected politicians to lie and think that's okay?

White-Haired Genius

The hair on my head that hasn't turned loose has turned white, which I've learned is a good thing. According to my grandkids when they were little, the reason their Grampa is very wise is "because he has white hair." Now I have a reputation to uphold.

Wisdom is worth more than silver and gold, more precious than jewels. Nothing else has so much value.
— *Proverbs 3:14–15*

Ten Thoughts to Ponder

1. I can understand many things, but I can't know anything compared to all the things I need to know, would like to know, or can know. Which is why I must trust the Lord.
2. Giving our lives to the Lord isn't enough if we think we should specify conditions for our surrender to his will.
3. After knowing what God *can* do, what he *will* do is a test of our faith until he does it.
4. Before I can set aside my misbeliefs, I must first want to know the truth—and then the Holy Spirit must show me what I couldn't see or understand.
5. God may know our thoughts, but it's much more important for us to discover God's thoughts.
6. Why pray? That's a question often asked, perhaps not easily answered, which might explain why we need to pray.
7. I must know that God makes me "good enough," or I will never be "good enough."
8. Wasting time might be important so the loss can remind us that time is short—so we shouldn't be wasting time.
9. The more times I can commit to God's timing, the more perfect my timing will be.
10. In letting the light of God shine through us, we reveal an opportunity for others, which cannot be described in words.

Questions for Further Thought

- What does it mean to be too smart for our own good?
- How can we know what we need to know when we don't even know what questions to ask?

Pied Piper

According to tradition, the pied piper played an hypnotic tune, and all the rats followed him to their death in the river. But when the king refused to pay him as agreed, the colorfully dressed musician led all the children away, never to be seen again.

More than seven hundred years later, people still follow the tunes that sound good, blind to the dangers that might lie ahead.

Jesus said to the people, "I am the light of the world. Those who follow me will never walk in darkness, because they have the light of life."
— John 8:12

Ten Thoughts to Ponder

1. To know God better, we must be much more interested in truth rather than tradition.
2. With the Lord, the best balance we can acquire in life is to have his strength in opposition to our weakness.
3. When we say we have no choice, we have ruled out all the alternative choices as unacceptable.
4. We should be thankful that God made us with a spirit capable of recognizing his presence—or be fearful when we want to go our own way.
5. I can be forgetful, but I forget why that is so often true.
6. For as long as I choose to deny reality, I make it impossible to accept the change that God would like to work in me.
7. With more of God's presence, we can find pleasure in anything, even in the pain and suffering.
8. If beauty is in the eye of the beholder and I want to see true beauty, then I need spiritual insight that only God can give.
9. Spare time is everywhere, hiding among all the work that must be done.
10. Today presents sufficient challenges with little time to regret anything about the past or worry much about the future.

Questions for Further Thought

- What leadership qualities can lead down a harmful path?
- How can people develop the critical thinking skills necessary to resist the influence of a bad leader?

Great Mistakes

I've learned to be thankful for my uncanny ability to make mistakes. Why? For one thing, if we're not making mistakes, we're not learning, and we're not accomplishing much.

In striving to *do* our best, not *be* the best, we can be thankful for our weaknesses because God's strength and wisdom can be revealed.

> *God uses what the world regards as foolishness to embarrass those who think they are so smart. Through our weaknesses, he will do mighty things that confound those who hold positions of power.*
> — 1 Corinthians 1:27

Ten Thoughts to Ponder

1. In walking with the Lord, we can be prepared, even when we don't know what's coming.
2. Compared to what God sees, I would be almost blind if he didn't help me see what I need to see when I need to see it.
3. If at any moment, we fail to walk with the Lord, we cannot know the value of what we missed.
4. When I have neither the knowledge nor the means to do the work, I am totally dependent upon the Lord.
5. We need more of God—not just for us, but to fulfill the purpose God has for us to help others.
6. Drowning in discouragement, we can be encouraged by knowing that God doesn't want to leave us there.
7. The best way to describe the indescribable is to say we don't know how to describe it.
8. Knowing what people are going to do gives God tremendous power to manipulate the outcome without violating their free will.
9. I think I was thinking when I didn't know what to think.
10. People who fake it with the hope of making it have a poor chance of ever making it without God's help.

Questions for Further Thought

- Why are people paralyzed with fear of making a mistake?
- How can preparation help us reduce mistakes, yet embrace them when they inevitably happen?

Connect the Dots

At age three, I had to find one dot and draw a line to the next number in sequence. This was not an easy task, but the great reward for my hard work was seeing the finished picture.

God is the artist who has my numbers, so I have to follow the Lord step-by-step. I don't mind, because I think the great reward will come when I see his finished picture.

> *From the beginning, I told you what the end would be. What hasn't happened yet will surely happen, and I will accomplish my purpose.*
> — Isaiah 46:10

Ten Thoughts to Ponder

1. Our greatest efforts are meaningless if they don't accomplish what God wants to work within us.
2. Human duplicates can't start to match the quality of God's originals.
3. Religion creates an illusion of righteousness without the reality of God's presence and the process that changes us to be like him.
4. With so many tools at our disposal, we need God's guidance to know which tools to use right now to fulfill his purpose.
5. A treasured thought that isn't recorded is an easily lost value.
6. If we have any interest in doing what God wants, we should be desperately seeking his guidance.
7. "Simply said" is seldom "simply done."
8. Being impulsive leads to thoughtless, silly actions—except when God is the force behind the impulse.
9. The purpose of the past becomes known when we meet the future.
10. When Jesus said a little faith can move mountains, he was talking about our trust in what God wants to move, not necessarily what we *think* should be moved.

Questions for Further Thought

- How can we make sense out of what doesn't make sense?
- What advice would you give to frustrated people who can't connect the dots in their lives?

Apple Core

I assumed Timmy Cox didn't want my apple, which already had a big bite out of the side, so I grabbed another apple and gave it to him. In less than a minute, he consumed the apple, core and all. Why did he eat the core? I was amazed.

I had always thought the core was something to be thrown away. But if it weren't for the core, we would have no seeds and no apple trees. Without the cores, there would be no apples.

> *Unless we believe in God and the rewards that follow, we'll neither approach him nor seek to please him.*
> *— Hebrews 11:6*

Ten Thoughts to Ponder

1. We would do well to set aside some necessities so we can do other necessities that are *really* necessary.
2. I must do my best with what I have, because I can't do anything with what I don't have.
3. The more of God's personality that I gain, the more I can be comfortable in my own skin.
4. *Nothing* is better than anything whenever *nothing* is what God wants.
5. Doubting can be good or bad, so we need God's help to distinguish exactly what we should believe.
6. All my downtime could be up time if I would focus my thoughts upon the Lord all the time.
7. If belief in the reward is lost, the effort cannot be justified.
8. The value of answers received depends on the quality of the questions we ask.
9. Spending a lot of time to learn ways to save time is a wonderful way to accomplish what we never thought we had enough time to do.
10. For me to experience the greatest pleasures in life, I must become God's great pleasure.

Questions for Further Thought

- Why might we easily overlook the most important things?
- How can we see the good that God sees but we don't?

God Speaking

Some Christians say God never speaks to them. Others talk like he's constantly calling on their cell phones. In his book *Let There Be Light*, blind author Joe Giovanelli describes his struggle to hear the Lord.

The last time I prayed for sight, I heard God speak to me, "Joe, it's best that you do not see. You will glorify me far more by being blind and showing that you have a full life. When you show people your love for me by word and action, I will be glorified."

> *If you have an ear to hear, you should listen.*
> — Revelation 3:13

Ten Thoughts to Ponder

1. One wrong conclusion can lead to many misconceptions that appear to be right.
2. If the painful process of life wasn't important for the fulfillment of God's purpose, everybody would already be in either Heaven or Hell.
3. Our priorities are easily followed when we change our rules and principles to whatever we want.
4. A great title won't sell a million books, but selling a million will make a book's title great.
5. Since God's thoughts are immeasurably greater than mine, I fight a losing battle trying to fully understand his plan and purpose—but it is fun to try.
6. An early finish requires an early start and relentless plodding.
7. Free will demands that we have a choice, but there can be only one best, right choice that is most pleasing to the Lord.
8. The opportunity to help others can make life worth living.
9. People are often concerned about how they look, but God is most concerned about how we are—on the inside, not just the outside.
10. Anything we get to do in Heaven is worth doing on Earth.

Questions for Further Thought

- How is God's voice distinguished from others?
- What might lead people to think God has never spoken to them and never will?

Monsters

In response to my crying, Daddy wrapped his arm around me and assured me that no monsters were under my bed. "Let's go look," he said. Nothing was hiding behind the curtains. While holding my hand, he walked with me into the blackest darkness.

My father's presence changed my perception of reality.

When I know the Lord walks with me, I have no reason to fear.

As I walk through the most trying times of my life, a dark valley of the shadow of death, I still don't have to fear, because you're at my side.
— Psalm 23:4

Ten Thoughts to Ponder
1. I can be grateful for God's ways, even when I don't understand them.
2. We shouldn't be so comfortable with where we are that we don't want to be where God wants us to be.
3. Motivated to do God's will, we won't be fired—but we can often be reassigned.
4. The greatest problem with finding solutions is knowing symptoms while being unaware of the root problem.
5. Good advice has no value unless we *see* its value, *test* its merit, and *do* it.
6. The future cannot be seen by looking back, for God is always in the business of doing new things.
7. Were it not for the sacrifice involved, commitment wouldn't have much meaning.
8. Incorrect assumptions lead to all kinds of erroneous thinking, with senseless conclusions that only seem to make sense.
9. Mountains are often moved one shovel at a time.
10. Treasure hunters endlessly search rubble with a faint hope for something of great value, but God is always present, waiting to be found.

Questions for Further Thought
- Why do people fear dangers that are improbable if not impossible?
- How can we comfort those who are paralyzed with fear?

Bible Belt

The pain of a spanking taught me obedience. My father's discipline was for my good, not my harm. His claim that my spanking hurt him more than me was true. Being obedient in all things, I loved him so much that I didn't have to fear him. We were bestest friends.

If the fear of the Lord is the beginning of wisdom, love is the end. As I walk with him, nothing is left for me to fear.

> *The fullness of our love for God leaves us no reason to cringe in fear of him. That's because the fear is based on our anticipation of his punishment, which is impossible when our love in him is complete.*
> — 1 John 4:18

Ten Thoughts to Ponder

1. As we walk with the Lord, we can accomplish a lot without even knowing how, for he is the great enabler.
2. If we are who God wants us to be, then by our own nature, we will do what he wants us to do.
3. I can think I was wrong and be wrong about thinking I was wrong, but I can always be right in thinking God is right.
4. It is never comfortabe to realize that one has been a fool, but it's the first step toward gaining wisdom.
5. A desire to believe or not believe has an uncanny ability to ignore the evidence and miss the obvious.
6. I need more patience, and I need it right now.
7. Like a ladder has only one top rung, we can have only one most-important action for what is most pleasing to the Lord.
8. When pleasing people is most important, we separate ourselves from God.
9. If we can't admit our need for God, we're not likely to want or receive what God has for us.
10. Impossible starts wait for the right time. Weak starts miss seeing the value of the process. Tragic starts come as soon as we quit. The only bad starts are those that teach us nothing.

Questions for Further Thought

- What keeps us from appreciating God's discipline?
- What is the difference between fear and reverence?

Worthy of Praise

As Jesus approached Jerusalem, a joyful crowd of followers cheered and shouted praises for all the miracles they had seen, saying, "Blessed is the king sent by God, who brings peace. Let the heavens rejoice and God be glorified."

Some Pharisees complained, saying, "Teacher, you should rebuke your followers for saying such things."

"You can be certain," Jesus said, "that if they kept quiet, the stones would have to shout praises."
— *Luke 19:40*

Ten Thoughts to Ponder

1. Live within your means, and you'll always have enough.
2. The power of Jesus' miracles came from his passion to do nothing out of his own initiative, but to act only as the Spirit led.
3. Without excitement, the groove we run in will feel like a rut.
4. We need God's help to know what we don't know but need to know, or we will be like the blind who fall into the ditch.
5. Pray without ceasing, not to have what we want but to have what God wants.
6. Some people dress in tatters to conceal their riches while others dress lavishly to conceal their poverty.
7. Impossibilities are achieved one possible step at a time.
8. Patience should turn our focus away from impatience by ignoring what we don't have and making use of what we do have.
9. For our ultimate goal to have meaning, we must know exactly where we are and the direction we need to go for the next right step.
10. One of the most important parts of action is knowing when to wait and when to move forward.

Questions for Further Thought

- What are our best reasons for praising the Lord?
- When we don't *feel* like praising the Lord, what can we do to change the feeling?

Unashamed

Everybody else in my third-grade class brought their lunches in a paper sack. Mom insisted I take cold milk and hot soup in a lunchbox shaped like a barn. The kids would tease me for sure, but I decided to act like I liked it. Strangely, the ridicule never came.

The next Monday, the boy across the aisle had a lunchbox like mine. So did Susie, Billy, and the tall kid in the back. That's when I knew I didn't have to be ashamed. People might follow my example.

> *I will not be ashamed when I share my story in public.*
> *— Psalm 119:46*

Ten Thoughts to Ponder

1. Perfection is being where God wants us to be, doing what he wants us to do.
2. When Jesus said, "It's finished," he was looking at an eternity of work left to do because of what he had finished.
3. We become a living miracle as God changes us.
4. Seeing God's reality instead of our own gives us a solid foundation upon which we can build something that lasts.
5. When busy about doing what God wants, we can do what otherwise we could not do.
6. God's gift of life is not to be restrained or contained, but it is to radiate his glory for everyone to see.
7. Having what God wants should be the perfect answer to having everything we want.
8. We need God's help to distinguish opportunities from obstacles, because with our limited eyesight, they can appear much the same.
9. Asking the Lord opens the door to receiving what he wants for us, but otherwise, asking closes the door because we want something else.
10. Imposters strive to look their best, but they must deal with the reality of not being who they appear to be.

Questions for Further Thought

- What causes people to be ashamed?
- Why are some people reluctant to share their testimonies?

Secret Service

At a Japanese grill, my friend and I prayed just before our meal was served. Obviously, we were Christians. As it turned out, so were the ladies on my left. Their conversation suddenly changed from partying and drinking. These three schoolteachers worked together, but they didn't know they were Christians until that day.

If you don't want to be noticed, look and act like everybody else.

> *If anyone publicly acknowledges me before men, I will publicly acknowledge him before my Father in Heaven.*
> *— Matthew 10:32*

Ten Thoughts to Ponder

1. The glory of walking with the Lord is greater than any pain we might endure.
2. The process is an unavoidable necessity for accomplishing everything God wants to work in our lives.
3. Our determination is destructive when it isn't submitted to the Lord's guidance.
4. A problem to solve. A question to be answered. A goal to achieve. A pleasure to pursue. A job to be completed. All worthless without the Lord.
5. Pleasing the Lord is good, but becoming the person he wants is better.
6. Being created for God's good pleasure is an indescribably wonderful thing, but only if we're willing and obedient.
7. Stupid mistakes make us smart when they lead us to abandon wrong and do what is right.
8. Being close to God requires walking with him, not expecting him to walk with us according to our direction.
9. People will pay for what they want, but you can't even give them what they don't want.
10. Since God is light and life, anything we say or do that takes us away from God must lead toward darkness and death.

Questions for Further Thought

- What gives people boldness to share Christ?
- What do we gain by hiding our light?

Fight or Flight

I never liked snakes, so I was surprised to learn that Jesus said I should be like one. Why? For sure, *not* to strike others with venomous fangs. He gave a metaphor for not inviting a fight and fleeing to avoid one.

We need not argue, because that wouldn't convince anyone. Just be eager to tell your story of how God changed your life.

> *Be wise as snakes, slipping in unnoticed, and harmless as doves, fleeing when threatened.*
> *— Matthew 10:16*

Ten Thoughts to Ponder
1. We are smart to anticipate and recognize the mistakes made by Artificial Intelligence.
2. If the exhortation to reckon ourselves dead daily is important, then we should also anticipate the need for daily resurrection.
3. "All I can do" is actually much more than "all I can do"—if I can have the Lord's help in all I do.
4. When Jesus prayed, "Not my will but yours be done," he was expressing his total commitment to pay the high price for what God wanted.
5. To accept God's ways, we must know they are better than all alternatives.
6. With my own creativity, I can produce a mess, but with the certainties that God provides, I can proceed with confidence.
7. A new discovery of truth is exciting because we didn't know it has always been true.
8. We could prove the effectiveness of prayer if we knew how to evaluate the results from God's perspective.
9. Walking with God, we can see no finish line, because there is no end to eternity with him.
10. If it weren't for the unknown that only God knows, we would be deprived of a wonderful, interesting adventure.

Questions for Further Thought
- How can we know when to persist and when to give up?
- Why do people respond differently to stressful situations?

Honestly

I said I didn't know where Daddy's fishing knife was, but later I remembered using it to build a dugout by the fence. I found the now-rusty knife and left it on the porch, not wanting to admit my fault.

Later, Daddy said to me, "You could have come to me. I would have understood."

> *The fullness of our love for God leaves us no reason to cringe in fear of him. That's because the fear is based on our anticipation of his punishment, which is impossible when our love in him is complete.*
> *— 1 John 4:18*

Ten Thoughts to Ponder
1. Please God with what you have, because you can't please God with what you don't have.
2. If we can't hear well, we can't know whether we are speaking well, so we do need God's help with our hearing.
3. God's presence is the greatest of all gifts, which we should treasure more than anything else.
4. We can be sure God will do what he wants within the boundaries of what he *can* do, because he already has and already is.
5. Walking in the presence of God can answer all the questions that we don't even know to ask.
6. When the cold days are gone, the roses will bloom again.
7. Wisdom comes when we can see beyond our doctrines and know how life really is.
8. If we're looking for guidance from the Lord, we should do everything possible to maintain a good connection with his presence, or we are likely not to hear anything.
9. Without our desire to please the Lord, his direction doesn't help us much.
10. Unbelief misses the truth for lack of desire, and misbelief misses the truth because it isn't yet known.

Questions for Further Thought
- What keeps people from being open and honest?
- How might dishonesty affect self-worth and relationships?

Better than Best

I did my best to do my best. I paid attention in class and excelled, academically. As a "promising" student, teachers encouraged me to pursue various vocations. I dreamed of being the best of the best in several professions. None of those would be worth anything if it wasn't what God wanted. So I chose wherever God might lead.

For life to be worthwhile, we need only do our best for him.

> *People who put to good use what they have will gain more, but people who do nothing with what they have will lose what they have hidden.*
> *— Matthew 25:29*

Ten Thoughts to Ponder
1. Those who are anticipating retirement should know that we'll never retire from whatever God has for us to do.
2. Encouragement has no value if it doesn't consider reality.
3. Salvation requires total surrender to God's will, for which we give up everything to have what he knows we need.
4. To enjoy our liberties, we need to get out more.
5. Showing excitement all the time would be really wonderful, because God is so wonderful all the time.
6. Success is easy if you can avoid all the pitfalls, and we need God's help for that.
7. The Creator of the Universe knows our thoughts and heart's desire before we pray one word.
8. Knowledge and understanding without the direction of the Holy Spirit is like having tools with no clue as to how they should be used.
9. We can always do our best now, with no need to wait until later.
10. The Lord's Prayer is much more than a roadmap of what to say, for it is all about focusing our desires in total surrender to God and having his benefits from doing that.

Questions for Further Thought
- Why are some people never satisfied?
- Why did Jesus need to tell people to let their light shine?

Baby Steps

Upstairs in Grandma's apartment, I took wobbly steps toward my Aunt Belva, her hands reaching out to help me if I should fall. It was a breakthrough moment when I was a year old, which I cannot forget. Today, I am still learning to walk with the Lord.

Walking and running with the Lord is good, but we shouldn't overlook our baby steps and our wayward steps that need his direction.

The steps of righteous people are directed by the Lord, and they love to walk with him. They may stumble, but they won't fall flat, because God will help them up.
— Psalm 37:23–24

Ten Thoughts to Ponder

1. If I can believe what my Father says is true, I can avoid the curiosity that would get me into trouble.
2. We choose whether we will be part of the good God is doing or the evil that he allows.
3. With the Lord, I can be content with better, because that will ultimately and inevitably take me to the best and the bestest.
4. If our time belongs to the Lord, we should never want to see it wasted.
5. I must know what God wants me to do, how to do it, and have the desire to do it—or it probably won't be done.
6. My imagination is insufficient to comprehend God's truth.
7. Knowing we don't understand can open the door to our hearing and believing the truth—if we listen to what the Lord is speaking to our hearts.
8. My best can never be good enough unless I have God's help.
9. God's presence makes goodness available to everyone.
10. If we love the Lord, we can know where we will be a hundred years from now—wherever God wants us to be, doing whatever he wants us to do.

Questions for Further Thought

- What can we do to improve our walk with the Lord?
- How can God guide us when we don't know him?

Rejection

My ninth-grade English teacher told my class to write a one-page story, so I wrote about a man who was marooned on the moon. On his return to Earth, his ship crashed, and he died.

I received an A+ from the student who graded my paper, but the next morning, the teacher held my paper before the class marked with a very large grade F.

> *I take pleasure in weakness, insults, and hardships. Persecuted, frustrated, suffering for Christ's sake, I am thankful for my weakness that makes me strong in him.*
> *— 2 Corinthians 12:9*

Ten Thoughts to Ponder

1. Instructions have no value if we insist on our own way.
2. We have no benefit in receiving God's presence if we are not givers of who he is in us.
3. "What God knows is better" is always better than "what I *think* is better"—unless I'm thinking like God is thinking.
4. God's instructions are an opportunity to hear him and do what is right—but only if we want to.
5. If we think we should see more miracles, we might question whether the faith formula we *think* is right is *really* right.
6. Without a desire to be better with God's help, we can easily become worse.
7. I would much rather have God's direction in what he wants than to have his permission to do what I want.
8. Perfection is not what we think it is, but it is whatever precisely matches God's purpose for us.
9. Robbing Peter to pay Paul can't make Peter happy, but Paul will be delighted and want to know why he can't have more.
10. The power behind miracles is being used of God, not using God.

Questions for Further Thought

- How can we use rejection to strengthen our faith?
- Why might our hurts keep us from moving forward in God's plan for us?

Missing the Obvious

"Who stole my glasses?" my science teacher said, looking around, obviously frustrated. "I'm not giving this test until somebody returns my glasses."

Nobody seemed eager to take the test. On his own, he would have to discover that his glasses were perched above his forehead.

> *Christ is the visible image of our God whom we otherwise could not see, who preceded all creation.*
> *— Colossians 1:15*

Ten Thoughts to Ponder

1. Until we die to self, we cannot really live as the Lord would have us live.
2. Before God can be in complete control of my life, I must completely surrender my desire to be in control.
3. Delight in the Lord has its greatest value when we can rejoice in the midst of hard times.
4. My prayer is for God to answer my desire with what he knows is best for me, not what I *think* is best.
5. Patience is doing all we can while waiting for the opportunity to do more.
6. The problem with sin is not the action, but it is the desire that is contrary to what God would have us do.
7. Our suffering is the evidence of our faith and the proof of our testimony.
8. There is no greater blessing than to be used of God on Earth, for with each good deed, we get a taste of Heaven.
9. I might be 80 percent right and 20 percent wrong, but I'm not sure which is the 20 percent.
10. Pursuing God's will is not merely a methodology, but it is a motivation to please him above our self-serving desires.

Questions for Further Thought

- How can our expectations prevent seeing what is right in front of us?
- Why are some people able to see what others cannot see?

Return on Investment

When you get to Heaven, what biblical character other than Jesus would you like to meet first? The typical answer is often Peter, Paul, or Abraham, sometimes David or Moses. What is my choice?

I want to talk to the elderly lady in the Temple who gave all she had. The Law didn't require that, so why did she do it?

> *I consider everything that hinders my knowing the Lord Jesus Christ as a total loss. I have sacrificed everything I had before, seeing it as garbage, so I could have the treasure that Christ has for me.*
> *— Philippians 3:7*

Ten Thoughts to Ponder
1. All of God's commandments are opportunities to experience more of his grace and glory.
2. Our next step can be crucial, because the slightest deviation from God's way could take us where we don't want to go.
3. When people see our actions, they should know that the Kingdom of God is here.
4. If we don't see the value of waiting, we won't do it.
5. The Good News is good only for the ones who hear, believe, and follow it.
6. Complete trust in God must reach beyond every reason we might have to doubt—so we believe anyway.
7. When we're walking with God, we get to experience one thrilling adventure after another.
8. Praise brings us closer to God, where we can abandon our wants and have what God wants.
9. When God doesn't explain his plan, we must trust him, step-by-step, and that's his plan.
10. With a little faith and a very big God, to be saved we need only to abandon our self-serving desires and follow Jesus.

Questions for Further Thought
- How do we balance meeting our personal needs with giving generously to God?
- What is the spiritual benefit of giving to the Lord?

Choice

I wasn't surprised when the man explained his plight and asked if I could help. I opened my wallet, thumbed past the smaller bills, and pulled out a twenty.

The next day, a man asked for help. "Sorry, I can't help you," I said. Why the difference? In the first case, I knew what God wanted.

> *By supporting one another in their areas of need, you fulfill the command of Christ.*
> *— Galatians 6:2*

Ten Thoughts to Ponder

1. Faith overcomes our reluctance to do God's will.
2. People may think asking is the magic formula for getting what they want, but trusting God for what he wants is much better.
3. What you do with your time and money reveals what you value most.
4. I won't waste much prayer time asking for what I want, because I think knowing what God wants and how I can fulfill his purpose is much more important.
5. If we can be thrilled by seeing God's blessings, then we don't have to be disappointed when we don't get what we want.
6. There's nothing better than a close-call accident to teach us to be more careful.
7. God's omnipotence and the extent of his lack of control due to free will deserves careful consideration if we are to understand reality.
8. To reach out and take God's hands, we must first get up and take our baby steps toward him.
9. Misdirected worship is mostly noisy *fan*fare than it is heartfelt *God* fare.
10. To provide genuine help to meet people's needs, we must have God's guidance to know when, where, and how.

Questions for Further Thought

- How can we make good choices when we don't know for sure what is right?
- By what means can we know when a choice is worth the risk?

Evil

"Evil exists," Bill said. "God created all things. Therefore, God must be evil for allowing evil." Bill underestimated the power of God, who created beings with free will, the ability to say no to their Creator and go their own way. We cannot blame God for our bad choices.

Never say God is tempting you to do wrong, for God can do no wrong and his purpose is always good. People are tempted when their desires take them in a direction different from where God would have them go.
—*James 1:13–14*

Ten Thoughts to Ponder

1. Mountains of impossibility are climbed one possible step at a time.
2. For the love we most desire, we must seek to give, not get.
3. The only way to have everything you want is to only want everything that God wants.
4. If you want Satan to leave you alone, fully submit to the Lord and you give the monster no reason to hang around.
5. When Jesus said, "It is finished!" that was just the beginning of something much greater.
6. Walking and running toward the Lord is good, but we shouldn't overlook our baby steps and the wayward steps that need his direction.
7. Our failure to wait can leave us wishing we had.
8. To get where we need to be, the next step is all we need to know.
9. ChatGPT has no connection with God for revelation of absolute truth.
10. For the next right step, we must admit where we are and where we need to be—and then depend upon the Lord for direction.

Questions for Further Thought

- Why do different cultures and philosophies define evil differently?
- How does God use evil to suit his good purposes?

Battery Life

When I lack "go juice" to do God's will, my batteries must lack power. Or maybe I have a weak connection somewhere. When I don't have a spiritual voltmeter, how can I identify the problem and boost my energy? If I recognize the reward, I'll find the energy.

Unless we believe in God and the rewards that follow, we'll neither approach him nor seek to please him.
— Hebrews 11:6

Ten Thoughts to Ponder

1. We must experience a spiritual birth in Christ before we can bear spiritual fruit.
2. ChatGPT can be a valuable resource for brainstorming and research, but the mind of Christ provides a greater value than Artificial Intelligence.
3. John 3:16 tells what God did for us, and 1 John 3:16 tells what we should do for him.
4. With God, being humble is recognizing our smallness and his greatness, while we recognize our greatness because of what he wants to do with our smallness.
5. If a liturgy doesn't bring us closer to God, it's a form that separates us from him.
6. Many people expect today to be like yesterday, so they miss God's guidance, unprepared for what they don't expect.
7. Claiming God's promises without a true spiritual relationship with him is worthless.
8. If we want to see the Lord touch people's hearts, we must speak in obedience to the Spirit, from the heart, not the mind.
9. If you want to know God, you should learn as much as you can about Jesus.
10. When we are spiritually tired, sleep helps less than meeting with the Lord so we can soar in the Spirit as if we had the wings of an eagle.

Questions for Further Thought

- What common distractions hinder our focus on God's will?
- What are the best ways to boost our spiritual energy?

Walk with God

In our impersonal culture, we can say we know people if we remember their names or have a Facebook connection. But do we *love* them? Maybe a little, but to really care, we need a personal relationship that comes from shared experiences.

Knowing God's name isn't enough. We need to walk with him.

> *The steps of righteous people are directed by the Lord, and they love to walk with him.*
> *— Psalm 37:23*

Ten Thoughts to Ponder

1. Taking time to help others is a better gift than money.
2. Walking with the Lord would be a whole lot easier if we weren't trying to take so many steps at one time.
3. What Jesus has done for us is enough to equip us to do for others.
4. With encouragement, we press on, but all of that is foolishness unless the Holy Spirit is the force behind the pressing.
5. If you're concerned about your treasures being stolen, store them in Heaven.
6. If I am to be more deeply involved with the Lord, my involvement in other, less-important things must diminish.
7. We naturally look at our physical needs, but God knows our spiritual needs are much greater.
8. By continual doing of whatever needs to come next, by sunset we can be thankful for a productive day.
9. God will keep his promise to us if we keep walking with him, seeking to do his will.
10. Our powerful Creator can do anything, but only within the limits of his nature that can't change. He can't hate the sinner, love sin, or *force* us to be what he wants.

Questions for Further Thought

- How do daily habits influence our ability to walk closely with God?
- How do trying times shape your walk with God?

Kingdom Economics

Before I got married, I traded my gas-guzzling Pontiac Grand Prix for a new Volkswagen beetle. What I saved on the cost of gas paid most of my car payment. Those were "the good old days" when paying a quarter for a gallon of gas was paying too much.

In the economics of the Kingdom of God, the good days lie ahead as God continues to do new and greater things.

No suffering in this age would be considered with any significance if we could see the magnitude of glory that will be eternally revealed in us.
— Romans 8:18

Ten Thoughts to Ponder

1. The glory of the Lord working within us comes from the doing, not the having.
2. God is constantly building upon what he has done in the past in order to create an even greater future.
3. We should always be eager for the Lord to interrupt our thoughts with better thoughts.
4. If we can enjoy the kinds of thrills that God has in his people, our joy will rise above all earthly pleasures.
5. Stupidity requires no education.
6. When the heart isn't prepared by the Holy Spirit to do the work, then the body cannot function as well as it should.
7. The truth wears well when you get used to it.
8. The Bible gives us the *who*, *what*, and *when*, but the *how* remains a mystery until we have the Holy Spirit to do the miracles.
9. We've become a lot smarter when we realize that our *desires* are the enemy, not Satan or sin.
10. If we expect to run through a wall and leap over a troop, or the other way around, we will definitely need the Lord's help to get there.

Questions for Further Thought

- In the Kingdom of God, what does it mean to be wealthy?
- What does the Kingdom Economics teach about the purpose of work, and how does this differ from secular views of labor and productivity?

Aging Beauty

Instead of trying to look twenty years younger and be someone other than who we are, maybe we should consider how people are often awed by a unique picture of a rustic old barn with its broken-down farming equipment.

God sees great beauty in making us unique, not what the world says we should be.

> *I praise you, Lord, because of the awesome, unique way that you created me. You did wonderfully well, and my whole being knows and declares this truth.*
> *— Psalm 139:14*

Ten Thoughts to Ponder

1. Our vision can be a distraction, but God's vision will take us where we really need to go.
2. Since we are naturally so inept at self-improvement, we should constantly look for God's help to make us who he wants us to be.
3. While waiting, we shouldn't sit and do nothing.
4. We make a terrible mistake to let the past define us. No matter how good or bad it was, our future in Christ is indescribably better.
5. You'll never see Heaven's glory if you don't look up.
6. Empowerment is never a single-person venture, but it works in partnership with the one who empowers.
7. Practice is wonderful for as long as the Lord is the one who is helping our improvement.
8. When we are strengthened by the Lord, we can move mountains, but our own effort might be only enough to turn over a rock.
9. Listening to what God is *not* saying can be exhausting.
10. As our source of unlimited power, the Lord will supply all we need to help others—if we are willing and obedient.

Questions for Further Thought

- What factors provide a deeper appreciation of inner beauty?
- How does media affect our perceptions of beauty

Different by Design

I once carried a polished pebble in my pocket as a reminder. Both that stone and I were different from everything else on Earth, and that's a wonderful part of God's plan and purpose.

Molds and patterns produce duplicates in mass production, but God has no pattern to make two people *exactly* alike.

> *Lord, you are still our Father. We are the clay. You are the potter. We are the work of your hands.*
> — Isaiah 64:8

Ten Thoughts to Ponder

1. The unbeliever's dilemma isn't a lack of belief, but it is the need to dispel misbelief.
2. Your story will be the evidence of God's glory, if you allow his light to shine from within you, every step of the way.
3. Good works are actually dead works when they are self-driven, not God-driven.
4. Besides all who God is, there is all who God is not, which would be those who love themselves at the expense of others.
5. Inspiration is easily found, but only if we are looking in all the right places.
6. When we surrender our will to God, putting our future in his hands, we need only be concerned with what he would have us do today.
7. If the Bible is an instruction book, we need the Holy Spirit to understand what it says.
8. Embrace the dawn, because it presents an opportunity to accomplish something you've never done before.
9. With self-direction, I am sure to wind up in trouble, because I can't see what God sees.
10. Since God is an inexhaustible resource, the only way we can have too much of him is failure to give.

Questions for Further Thought

- Why might society pressure people to conform instead of celebrating their differences?
- What are the advantages and disadvantages of being different?

Canned Speech

"What's wrong with these green beans?" The taste was yukky, far from what I expected. As it turned out, "fresh cut" beans out of the can in Mom's pantry had a much different taste from the beans cut fresh from our garden. Like it or not, I had to eat the beans from the can.

I don't know anybody who likes what I have to say when I pull something out of the can. Fresh, spontaneous insights are better.

> *Be gracious with your stories, flavoring your message with that which will answer the hunger in everyone's heart.*
> *— Colossians 4:6*

Ten Thoughts to Ponder

1. Trusting God is easy when we get to know him really well.
2. Those who don't know God but say, "It's good to be alive," cannot imagine what it would be like to be alive in Christ.
3. Our expectations work against us when God has a better plan.
4. The great treasures from our heart are worthless for as long as they remain locked within—words not yet spoken to help others.
5. Waiting upon the Lord is walking *with* him as he leads, not running ahead or lagging behind.
6. We pray without ceasing, not to have our way, but to take advantage of every opportunity to encourage others to know the Lord.
7. The proof of our faith is in getting whatever God wants, not in getting what we want.
8. The idea that we can have our dreams is foolishness—unless they reveal where God wants to take us.
9. We do well not to complain when God gives us what we think we do not need.
10. Not knowing what lies ahead, we can still be excited beyond words when we know we are living in the center of God's will.

Questions for Further Thought

- Why might a scripted message have less audience appeal?
- What distinguishes boring messages from captivating stories?

Asking Questions

Curious, I asked my teacher a difficult question. Her dismissive stare said, *Don't you know I'm the teacher? I'm the one who asks the questions.* I'm pretty sure she didn't know the answer.

Now we live in an *information* age when any online question can return immediate answers. I think we do well, asking questions, but we need God's help to know which answers are right.

> *If you don't know the truth or how to apply it, then ask God, because he's eager to help and won't make you feel stupid.*
> — James 1:5

Ten Thoughts to Ponder

1. When I leap into the air, I fall to the ground, but when the Lord lifts me, I don't have to fall.
2. We can be confident in God's plan when we meet the conditions for him to work all things together for good.
3. God's way is the right way, because my way won't take me to where I want to go.
4. If we were aware of all the miracles that God has worked in our lives, then we probably couldn't count them all.
5. Without appreciation for God's process, I risk missing the goal that he has for me.
6. Some Christians don't have time for thanksgiving, because they're too busy praying for what they don't have.
7. We should be thankful for our scars left by the wounds that brought us closer to the Lord.
8. Walking with the Lord, we can have perfect peace—since we don't have to worry about the future or be concerned about the past.
9. In Christ, the more we give, the more we have to give.
10. God's peace defies understanding, because it is a spiritual gift that is not dependent upon human observation.

Questions for Further Thought

- How does asking questions encourage critical thinking and develop problem-solving skills?
- What role does humility play in being willing to ask questions?

Digging Deeper

One evening at my friend's house, I shared what I'd learned from my kindergarten teacher. "Earth is a giant ball, and if we dig straight down, we'll be in China." After fifteen minutes of serious digging with two tablespoons, we thought we were making good progress.

That was the day I learned that goals are good only if you're willing to do whatever it takes to get there. Otherwise, we'll quit as soon as we think we're wasting our time.

> *Athletes give their lives in strenuous training for a short-lived glory, but we strive for a reward that will last forever.*
> *— 1 Corinthians 9:25*

Ten Thoughts to Ponder

1. The direction of the Holy Spirit is the best antidote for ignorance.
2. Ignorance is the weakest excuse for accomplishing *nothing*, because we already know enough to do *something*.
3. Wondering may stumble upon an answer, but asking someone who knows is the better approach.
4. I am limited in my pace, unwilling to drag my feet or run too fast, because I dare not fall behind nor run ahead of God.
5. To identify a lie, we must question the validity of its apparent truth.
6. The miracle of God's presence working in us allows us to accomplish more than we were able to do.
7. Being captivated by God is liberating, not constraining, freeing us to do all that is good.
8. Our definitions of love are grossly inadequate to define the nature and magnitude of God's love.
9. Faith can recognize a miracle when it is nowhere in sight.
10. Knowing we can never be good enough, we can embrace the truth that *God working in us* is always good enough.

Questions for Further Thought

- How does seeking hidden truths impact personal growth and relationships?
- Why are obvious truths sometimes missed?

Connectivity

A long-distance call was once made by cupping your hands around your mouth and yelling as loud as possible. With modern technological advances, we still face the same challenge. You can call, but will anyone answer? If not, a connection can't be made.

I'm wondering how God feels about this, because he's been calling since the beginning of time, waiting for people to pick up.

Lord, when I dial 9-1-1, you should know I'm in trouble and need you to answer right away.
— Psalm 102:2

Ten Thoughts to Ponder

1. If we want to know the truth, we should ask lots of questions and reconsider our beliefs.
2. If people can ignore the reality of God's presence, their imaginations can make lies appear to be truths.
3. The blind leading the blind cannot avoid the ditch, but walking with the Lord keeps us safe.
4. An encyclopedia is filled with knowledge, but we need the Holy Spirit for intelligence and wisdom.
5. God uses trying times to lead us to repentance, not regret.
6. Determined to do whatever is most pleasing to the Lord, we make it possible to do even better tomorrow.
7. We need the light of God to see well, or we'll stumble in the darkness.
8. Being thankful for God's gifts is good, but being thankful for the *use* of his gifts for good is even better.
9. If I'm not doing what God wants, then my achievements have no lasting value.
10. We may not know how, when, or where, but the strength of our faith in surrender to God's desires must inevitably move mountains.

Questions for Further Thought

- What are the best ways to maintain an online connection with God?
- When is it best to speak up or to shut up?

Dystopia

In 1962 when school prayer was becoming illegal, I said, "The world will never be the same." After the terrorist attack in 2001, I said it again. Later, the pandemic of 2020 left people cringing in fear. Is our world falling apart?

God is in control, and he can change everything if he wants to. The day will come when he will.

> *The Son of Man will appear in the sky, and the people of the earth will mourn. They will see him arrive in the clouds, with power and great glory.*
> *— Matthew 24:30*

Ten Thoughts to Ponder

1. Failure to embrace God's purpose in a temptation will make us victims instead of victors.
2. Ceremonies and liturgies have no value without a spiritual relationship in Christ.
3. If we want to tell better stories, we need better mental pictures of what happened.
4. Wanting what God wants still requires patience to see how he will work through us to fulfill it.
5. The great danger of health and wealth is forgetting our need for the Lord in all we say and do.
6. We need testing to reveal our spiritual strengths and weaknesses so we can fully surrender to God's will for us.
7. The *relevant* truth often lies hidden behind the *assumed* truth, just waiting to be discovered.
8. If something isn't working, we should at least recognize that we don't yet understand how it should work.
9. I don't try to understand others, because I have yet to figure out myself.
10. The most important step toward hearing God better is to recognize that we aren't hearing as well as we could.

Questions for Further Thought

- How might technology support a dystopian society?
- What causes resentment, strife, violence, and war?

Board of Education

Over the school loudspeakers, I was called to the principal's office. I'd picked up a one-inch paper airplane and threw it back to the person who had thrown it at me—just as a teacher walked in.

The other participants in my crime were the student council president and the valedictorian of my class. We got off with a warning, but I was sure I'd get jail time if I ever did anything like that again.

> *Our struggle is not with people but with the forces that influence our desires. We are pressured by spiritual wickedness in high places of authority—social prejudices, government leaders who tell people what they want to hear, and the media that filters, distorts, and spins the "truth" to suit their agendas.*
> *— Ephesians 6:12*

Ten Thoughts to Ponder

1. If we ever feel lost, we need God's direction and his means to get there.
2. We deserve no credit for our strokes of genius, because we're not smart enough to be that smart without God's help.
3. I don't know anything unless God helps me know, and even then, I need his help to be sure.
4. Running from God is a race you never want to win.
5. We can always proceed with confidence when we know we have God's help.
6. Listening is a means to add quality to the quantity of time.
7. Good works in abundance give people reason to glorify God in Heaven.
8. Satan is no more than a dark cloud trying to obscure the light of God's Son.
9. We should know that God will always give us strength to do what he wants.
10. Invention is useless without perception of a need.

Questions for Further Thought

- Why might discipline be important for effective teaching?
- When does correction become cruel and unreasonable punishment?

It's Greek to Me

Ancient Greek texts have no chapter breaks, numbered verses, or paragraphs. All letters were capitals, with no space between the words. YETPEOPLECOULDSTILLFIGUREOUTTHEMESSAGE.

No matter whether scholarly works are considered translations or paraphrases, excellence is best measured by how well an interpretation agrees with what the author would say to us today.

The Spirit of truth ... he will guide you into all truth: for he shall not speak of himself; but whatsoever he shall hear, that shall he speak: and he will shew you things to come.
— *John 16:13*

Ten Thoughts to Ponder
1. If we allow the Lord to intervene in some small way, we can glimpse a small portion of how great he really is.
2. Moses' rod had unlimited value when it was used to fulfill God's purpose.
3. For effective prayer, we need to ask for what God wants and not be content with asking merely what we *think* he wants.
4. Couples marry to get, but those relationships won't survive without sacrificial giving.
5. Perfection is having what we want when it is exactly what God wants.
6. Apart from God's guidance, a choice between two actions gives me at least a 50-50 chance of being wrong, and I don't like those odds.
7. The *stupidity* reached through Artificial Intelligence can be much worse than we think.
8. The simplest target is seeing only the center of the bull's eye.
9. Cancer might kill you, but not as certainly as turning away from God.
10. Listening is crucial for the sharpening of the mind.

Questions for Further Thought
- What can people do to overcome communication barriers?
- How might personal prejudices affect our ability to understand what others mean?

Wonderful Words

Before electricity, people worked by sunlight and read books at night by lamplight. People prayed for rain and a good harvest. When that didn't happen, we still had no better place to turn than to the Lord.

We're still hungry for good news, so we will always need songs of praise to remind us of God's goodness and why we have hope.

> *Are you suffering? Then turn to the Lord in prayer. Are you joyful? Then turn to the Lord in praise.*
> — James 5:13

Ten Thoughts to Ponder
1. Sometimes I need to remember what I know, so I go back and revisit God's miracles so I can have the right anticipation for what lies ahead.
2. We will suffer writer's block when we try to replicate God's voice from the resources of my own minds.
3. Hearing God goes far beyond the physical capacity of our ears and must touch our spiritual sense of knowing.
4. I thought I knew—until I realized that I didn't know as well as I thought I knew.
5. Questions lead to discovery because they encourage desires to learn what we might need to know.
6. Without an *emotional* choice, *information* won't lead to *transformation*.
7. If Job had seen God's purpose in his suffering, his complaining would have turned to exuberant praise.
8. Boasting about God's gifts cannot be very smart, for that is what Satan did before his downfall.
9. Since we can be sure God will have his way, it would be a very good idea not to hinder whatever he wants to do.
10. If we think time is valuable, we should spend it wisely and never waste a drop.

Questions for Further Thought
- How do encouraging words affect someone's wellbeing and confidence?
- Why might people underestimate the power of their words?

One by One

In the Great Depression, many people didn't have jobs and did well to keep from starving. Some remembered the 1897 song to "count your blessings, naming them one by one" and still had plenty to be thankful for because they didn't spend time counting their lack, one by one.

Jesus said getting more depends upon our giving more. Maybe if we were more thankful for what we have to give, we'd experience the blessing of giving and have more blessings to count.

> *The measure you give determines the measure you will receive.*
> *— Luke 6:38*

Ten Thoughts to Ponder

1. Preaching to the choir might be a very good thing when we don't know the right song to sing.
2. If we're looking for spiritual answers in the physical realm, we'll never find what we're looking for.
3. Love is a many-splendored thing when we get to give what we have been given.
4. When Jesus said none are good but God, he was saying the only way we can be good is to be an expression of who he is.
5. To love righteousness, we must hate our unrighteousness, which requires heart surgery.
6. We do well to abhor religion as an empty form, void of power, but to embrace God's reality with our whole being.
7. God's tests reveal whether our faith is as real as we think it is.
8. In knowing God's truth, logic may recognize the power, but emotion decides to flip on the switch.
9. Understanding the *pattern* of salvation is a far cry from the *practice* of salvation.
10. Having exhausted all the things that don't work and admitting our inability, we have a much better opportunity to discover what *will* work with God's ability.

Questions for Further Thought

- Why do people focus on losses instead of their blessings?
- How can we encourage someone struggling with losses or hardships to focus on their blessings?

Feasting

For many, holidays are about not having to work, being with family, eating too much, and watching sports on TV. Feasting is good, but I'm thinking relationships should be more than meat, potatoes, and pie.

We can enjoy our greatest feasting times together when we invite the Lord's presence, as we join in fellowship at the dinner table.

> *Don't be like some who fail to regularly meet together. Encourage one another more and more as the day of the Lord's return approaches.*
> *— Hebrews 10:25*

Ten Thoughts to Ponder
1. Since I don't fully understand me, I doubt I can fully understand anything *outside* of me.
2. God's revelation alone is like a dictionary on the shelf, not benefiting anybody until it is read, understood, and applied.
3. We must never make Satan's mistake and try to steal God's glory for ourselves.
4. Joseph had dreams that appeared to be nightmares until after God's purpose for all the tragedies had been revealed.
5. If we had God's perspective, we would never question his actions.
6. The miracles we want will be different from what God does, because he knows much more that what we know.
7. Without understanding God's purpose, we need faith to know how our tragedies could have a good purpose.
8. To understand who we are, why we are here, and what we are to do, we need to hear God's voice—because he's the one who knows.
9. Since I am not in control, but God is, I am in no position to answer my own questions.
10. To be energized, people need church, fellowship, and devotions, but we most need to bask in God's presence for a very long while.

Questions for Further Thought
- How does eating together strengthen relationships?
- What can we do to make people feel welcome?

Learning from My Father

My father was the same person at home as the preacher he was when he stood before the congregation at church. I'm sure his discipline and advice by example were an essential part of my coming to know the Lord, saving my life.

"A weak Christian," he said, "wants to hear a word from the Lord. A strong Christian already knows the word of the Lord, because he's always listening."

Teach your children right from wrong, and as adults they will make good choices.
— Proverbs 22:6

Ten Thoughts to Ponder

1. We will struggle with God's answers when they don't agree with what we want to believe.
2. Searching for truth, we will not do well at finding—unless we have God's help to look in all the right places.
3. Each retelling of a story deepens the life-changing experience.
4. In our ignorance, we would be really smart not to doubt God—if we are smart enough not to doubt.
5. Growth is crucial, because without it, we're dying.
6. Doing God's will requires a change of appetite to please the Lord and detest any thought, feeling, or action that wouldn't please him.
7. If God could and doesn't, then he must have a purpose in *not* doing what we think he should.
8. Unless I can appreciate what others are thinking, what I'm thinking can't matter to anyone but me.
9. If we can identify Satan's temptations as being harmful and potentially fatal, we will deny each one.
10. When feeling that our *desires* are not quite right, we can be sure that our *actions* aren't quite right, either.

Questions for Further Thought

- How might times with our earthly father affect our relationship with our heavenly Father?
- In what ways should we honor our father and also God?

Paying Attention

My Mom used to say I had "convenient hearing." I wish I could say she was wrong. But since I know she was right, I must push myself to listen better.

King Saul seems to have reasoned that God must be wanting what looked right to Saul. In contrast, David sought a change in his own desires so he would want whatever God wanted.

> *[People] have no excuse for not believing and doing the good they know to do, since the power and nature of our invisible God can be clearly observed in his creation.*
> *— Romans 1:20*

Ten Thoughts to Ponder

1. Worrying over what to say next can keep us from hearing what we must know before we can know what to say next.
2. People are like stained glass—most beautiful when God's light shines through.
3. Childlike people accept discipline, but childish people insist on their own way.
4. When people trust their ideologies or imaginations, they can miss God's reality and never know it.
5. The model prayer seeks total surrender to God's will so we can have all that is to be gained from that effort.
6. We *really can* be part of God's family, which is as wonderful as anything that has ever been created in the heavenly realm.
7. We should be dependent upon the Lord for everything, including our ability to do anything.
8. Faith in hearing and believing God's voice rises above hope to being sure of the truth without physical evidence.
9. Temptation leads us to do what looks good but isn't really for our good.
10. We pray and see doctors about our physical pain, but our greatest need is spiritual transformation.

Questions for Further Thought

- What is the difference between hearing and truly listening?
- What distraction keeps us from paying attention?

Taught to Pray

In the synagogue, Jesus' disciples learned the liturgy of prayer. John the baptizer taught spontaneous prayer from the heart. From Jesus, they learned the language of *spiritual* prayer.

I could ask my dad for anything, but he was good at giving me what I needed, not necessarily what I wanted. I have learned that effective prayer is more than simply asking and believing. I do best when I ask according to my Father's will.

> *The Holy Spirit will help us in our weaknesses. For example, we don't always know the Lord's will and what to pray for, but the Spirit prays through us with groaning that English words cannot express.*
> *— Romans 8:26*

Ten Thoughts to Ponder

1. We appreciate people who express gratitude for the good we've done, but hearing God say thank you is priceless.
2. A fragment of God's love is worth more than the fullness of ourselves.
3. Under Law, people went to the Temple to meet God, worship, and pray. But now, under Grace, *we* are his temple.
4. God's love is worth dying for—or we will die for something else.
5. Understanding how something works can involve separating the parts to see how each one functions with the others.
6. We should thank God for our bad days when they bring us closer to him.
7. Discomfort and confusion come from feeling we should do something when we really don't know if we should.
8. Preparation is doing it now because there won't be time to do it later, when it's needed.
9. When peace and quiet are difficult to find, we most need to hear the Lord in the midst of all the noise.
10. Without the night, we'd have no appreciation for the morning.

Questions for Further Thought

- When is it most important to pray?
- Why do some people pray as a "last resort"?

Our Creator

The Milky Way, a fraction of God's creative genius, takes my breath away. I am also awed by God's smallness, how he sees every sparrow that falls, is aware of every move I make, and even knows my thoughts.

Since a creator must always be greater than the created, our Creator God must be much more magnificent than anything we can imagine.

Creator of all things, you are worthy of all honor, power, and glory, because everything that exists was created for your good purpose.
— Revelation 4:11

Ten Thoughts to Ponder

1. I may not understand everything, but I do need to know what God knows I need to know, at the time I need to know it.
2. The obvious becomes invisible when we're looking in the wrong direction.
3. God will not take his people through difficult times without a good purpose that justifies the pain.
4. If we let him, Satan will steal what we need and give us what we don't need but might think we do.
5. Christians who think they are in control have missed the crucial truth about their need for God, for we can do nothing of value without his help.
6. *Closed* doors are as important as *open* doors when they take us to where God wants us to be.
7. If God knows when we're sleeping or awake, we should seek his dreams, which are so much better than our nightmares.
8. God's sense of humor points toward realities we might otherwise miss.
9. If we are as the Bible says, fearfully and wonderfully made, we're not a copy of anybody else. We should love our uniqueness in Christ, made different for his unique purpose.
10. Carrying God's burdens is much easier than trying to walk with sin's chains.

Questions for Further Thought

- What parts of creation make you feel closer to God?
- What does it mean to be "created in God's image"?

Heaven's Presence

I don't want to visualize God as distant, living somewhere beyond the stars, just barely able to hear my words. That's a misconception, since he's present everywhere.

As we continue to walk with him, God's presence allows us to experience much more of Heaven while we are still on Earth.

> *Is there anywhere I could escape your presence? If I go to the farthest region of space and beyond, you are there. If I am laid to rest in the deepest grave, you are there. If I had wings to fly with the dawn to reach the faraway seas, your hand would be there to guide me.*
> — Psalm 139:7–10

Ten Thoughts to Ponder

1. Since seeing the truth can't *force* us to believe, we must first *choose* to believe God before we can see his truth.
2. If people could see all that God is doing, they would either be thrilled or terrified.
3. When I am sure my imagination isn't creating God's voice, then I can know when I am really hearing him.
4. Fools feel compelled to share their thoughts when they have none.
5. One great difficulty in following God's direction is overlooking the little details that we *think* are unimportant.
6. *Simplicity* is having a single God-given focus, and *complexity* is trying to understand it all.
7. Since God knows me so much better than I know myself, he knows what I really need—and I can only guess.
8. The answer means nothing until we understand the problem.
9. Instead of helping, my message might be damaging—unless God helps me say the right thing, and that's assuming I am supposed to say something.
10. God hurts for lost people more than we can hurt for our losses.

Questions for Further Thought

- How can we become more aware of God's presence?
- How does sharing God's love connect us with him?

Hallowed Name

I'm trying to imagine what would happen if I said to others, "Glory to your name." It wouldn't make sense to them, and I understand why. It makes no sense to me. So now I'm wondering whether those words have meaning when I say them to God in song.

True love finds meaningful words, so I have to say those words might be useless in expressing feelings from my heart.

> *People will have to account for every word carelessly spoken. By your words, you will be either justified or condemned.*
> *— Matthew 12:36–37*

Ten Thoughts to Ponder

1. *Living* to fulfill the Lord's plan and purpose is more difficult than *dying* for him, because everybody will die for something.
2. The joy of the Lord has value when we find ways to express it.
3. I had a thought that I thought was really important until I thought otherwise, and now I don't know what to think.
4. Silence is golden when we can turn off the noise and hear God's voice.
5. When feeling *good* is based on thinking we are in control, we should feel *bad* because we haven't put God in control.
6. Problems are solved by confronting the issues, not by avoiding them.
7. Experiencing God's glory is a pleasure we can enjoy in continually greater measure for all of eternity.
8. Nobody but Jesus can calm the storms that rage within.
9. I sleep with my reading glasses nearby because I'll need them if I wake up and need to preserve an important thought that would otherwise be forgotten.
10. A rich man will have an abundance of cheap friends.

Questions for Further Thought

- How can we know when our words are helping, not hurting?
- When the truth hurts, what can we do to encourage and inspire others with our words?

Coming Kingdom

Before we can be citizens of God's Kingdom, we must recognize the phrase "King of kings and Lord of lords" as more than titles for Jesus. If he is our king, we respect his authority and will do what he says.

Usually, surrender is a sign of defeat, but in this case it's our only means to achieve victory in the Kingdom.

> *Unless your righteousness is greater than the righteousness of the Pharisees and teachers of the Law, there is no way you will enter the Kingdom.*
> — Matthew 5:20

Ten Thoughts to Ponder

1. With total focus on doing what God wants, we need not be concerned about the results, because we put the outcome under God's control.
2. For as long as we think we can make it on our own, we have no need for God's help.
3. Laws tell us what not to, which are more than we can remember, let alone do. But Love tells what is right to do.
4. A chemo infusion of God's instructions will cure the cancers of confusion and misbelief.
5. Since Scripture is so easily twisted to suit whatever we want to believe, we do best to hear him speak to our hearts.
6. If we want to see better, we should take a closer look in the Son light.
7. God's transformation process can be so gradual that I can't see any difference when I look in the mirror, but it's there.
8. Doing right in our own eyes is more likely wrong than right.
9. All my misbeliefs need to be sacrificed for the sake of the truth that God knows I don't know.
10. Without patience, we will miss God's promise, because we will wind up going our own way.

Questions for Further Thought

- How does U.S. citizenship differ from the Kingdom of God?
- What does it mean for "the Kingdom of God to come in power"?

Greater Reward

In training, Olympic athletes subject themselves to what most of us would consider unreasonable pain. Why? They do it for a chance to win the prize—a belief that their sacrifice will result in a great reward.

For the same reason, we should want God's will, no matter the cost, because a much greater treasure lies ahead.

> *My Father, if you are willing, let me escape this suffering. Nevertheless, I want your will, not mine.*
> *— Luke 22:42*

Ten Thoughts to Ponder

1. Before we *receive* God's forgiveness, we must recognize our wrong desires and repent, seeking not to be who we've been.
2. Writing is good if it works and bad if it doesn't, but our choice of words can always be made better.
3. When free from the desires of our self-serving flesh, we are free to enjoy the great spiritual thrill of pleasing the Lord.
4. Life's most important lesson teaches our need for God—if we're willing to learn.
5. God works with every person on Earth in a different way, because each of us is a special creation, called to fulfill a unique purpose.
6. As we surrender our lives to him, God can make miracles out of our messes.
7. God deserves our very best, and with his help, doing our best is always better than anything we could do on our own.
8. Temptation is the opportunity to believe and do something other than what we know is right.
9. I can choose to enjoy the most difficult, trying part of life, which is *finishing*—not the easy part, which is *starting*.
10. People are like stained glass, most beautiful when God's light shines through.

Questions for Further Thought

- How can we distinguish God's will from our desires?
- Where can we find joy and contentment when God's requires difficult and costly sacrifices?

Heaven on Earth

Amazingly, I have the power to say no to my Creator. Since God gave me free will, I could be like a strong-willed, obstinate child, crying for my way and throwing a tantrum when I didn't get it. Or I could believe the truth—that what God wants is always better than what I want.

I'm always better when I have what God wants. That's why I keep praying, "Please don't give me what I want if it's not what you want."

May your Kingdom come and your will be done, on Earth as it is in Heaven.
— Matthew 6:10

Ten Thoughts to Ponder

1. The right kind of asking will ultimately produce what God wants—and that will satisfy what I want, better than having what I want.
2. The more we fear, the more we make it true in our minds.
3. Instead of telling God what I want, which he already knows, I need to ask what he wants, which I don't always know.
4. Heaven can be called *home* only when that's where we belong.
5. Fulfilling God's vision is possible only after we have surrendered our vision and have embraced whatever he wants.
6. Hunger is wonderful when it seeks the Lord for satisfaction.
7. After recognizing a problem and discovering an answer, we still need God's help to say and do exactly what God wants.
8. God who is "out of this world" has a place for us that is "out of this world."
9. People have such a desperate need to be appreciated, they fret over what even their enemies think of them.
10. Instead of shouting, God often whispers so we will focus our ears and listen.

Questions for Further Thought

- How might our conversations with God bring aspects of Heaven into our earthly experience?
- What can a faith community do to help people enjoy more of Heaven on Earth?

Daily Worries

We buy insurance, save for retirement, and develop strategies to make our future secure. Then we worry about everything we can't control.

Do we really know him, putting what he wants first? If so, we need only be concerned with what he wants us to do today.

> *Do not trouble yourselves with questions like "What shall we eat ... drink ... or wear?" Seek first his Kingdom and his righteousness, and he will give you everything you need. Do not worry about tomorrow, for ... today's problems are enough for today.*
> *— Matthew 6:31, 33–34*

Ten Thoughts to Ponder

1. We need the work of the Holy Spirit to cleanse us from the inside, because our self-righteousness isn't good enough.
2. The most important part of my prayers is how they change me to be more like Jesus.
3. My surrender is the most crucial part of God's transformation process because that choice determines what he can do.
4. Salvation is about sinless living, not just avoiding Hell.
5. "Love" is a euphemism for something we don't know how to define, because the fullness of its meaning can only be understood as our relationship with the Lord intensifies.
6. When people have nothing to hide, they can always tell the truth.
7. Without God's help, I'm not smart enough to know what needs to be done, let alone how to do it.
8. My ignorance is a wide-open door for God to provide answers—but only if I'm listening to him.
9. There is no better pattern for perfect human behavior than what Jesus said and did when he walked on Earth.
10. The most important answer to hear from God is to know that everything is going to be all right.

Questions for Further Thought

- What steps will help us avoid worrying about tomorrow?
- What should people be most worried about today?

Amazing Generosity

Our Pledge of Allegiance says we want "liberty and justice for all." Yet a study of our legal system will say our ability to achieve that goal is far from perfect. Could it be that God has a better way?

As I consider my past, I don't want what I deserve. I want to be forgiven, so maybe I should be more forgiving.

> *If your enemy is hungry, prepare a feast for him. If he is thirsty, give him your best wine. Your generosity will amaze him—as much a shock as coals of fire being poured upon his head—and God will reward you.*
> *— Romans 12:20*

Ten Thoughts to Ponder

1. Exercise in God's Word is a great source of spiritual strength.
2. Life is found in the abundance of helping others, not in how much we have for ourselves.
3. What we don't know or understand must be left with the Lord to guide us, or we subject ourselves to confusion and frustration.
4. We'll never understand God's love until we've learned to share it.
5. We need God's help to let go of our regrets and worries about the future so we can enjoy his blessings today.
6. The world's ways look so right and good, we need the Holy Spirit to guide us to light and life.
7. Being "born again" is nothing to boast about if we've not grown to walk with the Lord, desiring only to please him.
8. Time may be short, but there is always time to be and do what God wants.
9. If people knew how much God cares, they wouldn't childishly think, when he doesn't give them what they want, that he doesn't love them.
10. Listening to what others think is more difficult than telling what we think.

Questions for Further Thought

- What motivates people to either be generous or selfish?
- How can we encourage forgiveness and generosity?

Ultimate Good

Some people think God allowing evil makes him evil. Actually, our freewill choices allow evil, yet God has ultimate control. He will use evil to accomplish his good purpose, as with the evil that Joseph endured to become chief in command in Egypt under Pharaoh.

We should pray for God's help to keep us from temptation and not be part of the evil that he allows for good.

> *People are tempted when their desires take them in a direction different from where God would have them go. Make no mistake, my friends, all that is good and fulfilling comes from God.*
> *— James 1:14, 16–17*

Ten Thoughts to Ponder

1. From the manger to the cross, Jesus' surrender to the Father's will revealed the way to eternal life with him.
2. From the human perspective, God's perfect plan can appear to be imperfect.
3. Confidence in our future rests on knowing God will use our efforts for good beyond anything we could do on our own.
4. The most difficult price I must pay to know God's truth is the sacrifice of all my misbeliefs.
5. Salvation is a transformation process that brings death to self-serving desires and resurrection life in our spiritual being to become like Christ.
6. Experience is the best teacher because what we learn is not easily forgotten.
7. The process of eternal growth in God's presence says there will always be more of his greatness to be experienced.
8. God has all the right answers all the time, even when we don't have all the right questions.
9. In believing wrong information, we are sure to be misguided unless the Holy Spirit leads us out of error into the truth.
10. Failure is never fatal unless we give up on God.

Questions for Further Thought

- How can our rationalizations justify good or evil actions?
- What can temptations reveal about our need for God's help?

Blame the Devil

Comedian Flip Wilson once said, "The devil made me do it," which people loved because any excuse is better than none. But no matter what my hardships have been, I can't truthfully say, "It's not my fault."

As a sinner, I wasn't forced to do right. As a righteous person, I'm not forced to do wrong. I can pray, "Deliver me from evil," but I need to remember that my choice depends on my desire, not God's.

Completely surrender your will to whatever God wants. Then your resistance to the devil is an absolute no, and he has no reason to hang around.
— *James 4:7*

Ten Thoughts to Ponder
1. Waiting on God should be about serving others, because he's not likely to equip us for work we're not doing.
2. With our eyes focused on the Lord, mountains can look like molehills.
3. We're getting smarter when we know we need help, and genius comes when God is our topmost resource.
4. Praise with heartfelt passion will reach the throne of God.
5. We should know that loving people is important, because Jesus said loving people is as important as loving God.
6. Obedience would be meaningless if it didn't come at great cost.
7. "All have sinned" says we all are foreigners—until we become sinless members of God's family.
8. Given our weaknesses, inabilities, and ignorance, our need for God should be obvious.
9. Christians who say, "I'm lucky to be alive," have the wrong message because our wellbeing isn't anything close to luck.
10. I think I'm not missing anything, which causes me to overlook what I am missing.

Questions for Further Thought
- What do people gain or lose by blaming the devil rather than taking personal responsibility?
- What are the dangers of identifying the wrong enemy?

Precious Process

When I was young, Daddy liked to say I'd probably get coal or straw in my Christmas stocking. I knew he was teasing. I *hoped* he was teasing. But had I been good enough to get the prize.

Since then, I've learned that the *process* is more important than the *prize*. Why? Without finishing the process, we don't get the prize.

> *Those who remain faithful until the end will be saved.*
> *— Matthew 24:13*

Ten Thoughts to Ponder

1. In the flesh, Abraham fathered stiff-necked, hard-hearted, Godless people, but in the spirit, he fathered a family of faith who heard God's voice, believed, and followed his direction.
2. Planting seeds is wasted effort without the water of the Word and plenty of Son light.
3. Jesus humbled himself in human flesh so the small percentage of people who received him could be made perfect and live with him forever.
4. *Stop* or *go* is what we need to do whenever God says to do one or the other.
5. When discouraged, we must first *want* encouragement. Then we can embrace God's encouraging words.
6. Counting time is good, but making time count is better.
7. When we say we have no time, what we actually lack is desire to cut the *unimportant* so we can do what's *important*.
8. Getting away isn't always good—unless we're sure God will walk with us.
9. *Confession* is what Judas did before hanging himself. *Repentance* is what Peter had when he wept bitterly after denying the Lord three times.
10. When the strain and pain seem so great, we need God's grace to set us straight.

Questions for Further Thought

- How might challenges and setbacks during the process prepare us for God's ultimate plan for our success?
- Why might understanding the process encourage others?

Good Deal

The pursuit of our dreams depends on our perception of value and cost. If the cost seems too high, we think we have a bad deal.

To have all of God, the cost is all of me. And that's a very good deal.

> *Those who have sacrificed their homes, relatives, or possessions for sake of the Kingdom will receive much more in this life and will have eternal life.*
> *— Luke 18:29–30*

Ten Thoughts to Ponder
1. Seeing our world from a perspective other than our own is virtually impossible without the help of God who sees all things.
2. Biblical authority doesn't make a verse true, but because it is true, we should accept its authority.
3. The Gospel brings a lifesaving message to some, but condemnation to those who choose not to listen.
4. In accepting Jesus, we must accept his way, his truth, and his life.
5. One day, the future will be greater than anything we can imagine, but in the meantime, we have work to do for the Lord.
6. God's smallest gifts are huge blessings when put to good use.
7. If the rich man had given up everything to follow Jesus, he'd have sacrificed a treasure in exchange for an abundance of life that is priceless.
8. Seldom is complacency recognized as a threat, because it just sits there, doing nothing.
9. People say dying takes believers to a better place, but actually, each arriving saint makes Heaven a better place.
10. We can give up on God, but his love won't give up on us.

Questions for Further Thought

- What factors should be considered when determining if an offer is a good deal?
- Why do people often buy what looks good but won't last?

Game Plan

As important as goals and strategies are, the odds of success are small if we blindly follow our plan. Why? Countless factors are beyond our control. Following God direction is always better, because he controls the results and can guarantee our success.

Trust God with your whole being, and don't rely solely upon what you think is true. Let the Lord guide everything you do, and he will keep you on the right path.
— *Proverbs 3:5–6*

Ten Thoughts to Ponder

1. When everything is going wrong, we have no better place to turn but to the Lord, who can make everything right.
2. The problems in our lives are too big for us to move by ourselves, but God moves mountains.
3. If we don't know what we really need, then we must look to God for help, because otherwise, we can't know what we're looking for, let alone where to look.
4. Having what we want is "happiness short-lived," but the joy of the Lord is an everlasting treasure.
5. Praying for more has little value when we've not yet put to good use the gifts and talents we already have.
6. The more we have, the more we need God's help to use our abundance of gifts for his glory.
7. Whatever God wants is my great pleasure, because whatever God doesn't want is my great displeasure.
8. We can choose not to complain—because we have plenty of reasons to be thankful.
9. The more we can treasure God's presence, the more we can be trained and transformed to who God wants us to be.
10. The opportunities to help others are endless—but only if we're looking for them.

Questions for Further Thought

- Why might people struggle with surrendering their plans to God?
- How can we know when we're going down the wrong path?

Generally Speaking

After a tornado cut a mile-wide path across the country, we would understand "complete devastation" to be *essentially* true. But we wouldn't be surprised if a few trees were still standing and all the houses weren't destroyed. One or two might be left untouched.

Jesus passed many afflicted people to reach whoever the Holy Spirit led him to. He didn't always heal them "all."

A great number of blind, crippled, and sickly people waited [and to one man, Jesus said,] "Pick up your mat and start walking."
— John 5:3–8

Ten Thoughts to Ponder

1. God's foundation beneath the surface must be finished before the next stage of his work, now visible, can be seen by those whose eyes are wide open.
2. We should want to be a blending voice in God's heavenly choir, not a standout.
3. Coveting what others have is a dangerous desire for something other than the glory that God has in store for us.
4. Pay attention to the little things because they are bigger than you think.
5. Everybody has a dictionary full of words, but we need God's help to arrange them in a message that will help others.
6. When we get to the end of our rope, it's time to let go and grab the Lord's hand.
7. With the Lord, we drive straight forward, without need for a rearview mirror to bring the past with us.
8. Feasting at the Lord's table gives us strength to do his work.
9. One of the most difficult communication skills that must be learned is when to be quiet, not saying anything.
10. Safety isn't escape from the storm. It's having Jesus with us, so the storm doesn't matter.

Questions for Further Thought

- Why might people interpret general statements as absolute truths?
- How might we benefit from the exception, not the rule?

Fact Versus Faith

Some facts don't change—like the low temperature yesterday. Facts may be conditional, such as the boiling point of water, which is 212 degrees at sea level and 160 degrees at the top of Mount Everest. Other facts are true only because we believe them, which is why diamonds are more precious than rubies and gold is worth more than silver.

True or not, what we believe plays a crucial role in our behavior, which is why we need the Holy Spirit to guide us.

> *Faith believes when physical evidence is lacking.*
> *— Hebrews 11:1*

Ten Thoughts to Ponder
1. Truth by extension says things equal to the same thing are equal to each other, but green apples aren't equal to green grass.
2. Soft words of wisdom are hard to shout against.
3. Without God's help, my understanding of reality is sure to include many assumptions and some misbeliefs.
4. I can talk in my sleep, which is one thing I can do that God can't do.
5. Great projects develop from imagination to discussion, implementation, and evaluation—on a path toward continuous improvement.
6. To have great thoughts, we need the mind of Christ.
7. Our society that loves its sleeping pills would do well to wake up and hear what God is saying now.
8. When looking for a mentor, God is our best choice.
9. Improvement is having less of anything I want when it might conflict with something God wants. Then I can have more of everything he wants.
10. We need not worry about our weaknesses when we have the Lord who is our strength.

Questions for Further Thought
- How can faith help us when the facts seem discouraging?
- What does it mean to walk by faith, not by sight?

Mother's Day

One day, I was amazed to hear that my ninety-year-old grandmother had been a bank manager. "Why did you quit the bank?"

Grandma smiled. "Because I married your grampa." In her day, only single ladies worked outside the home. Most people would say life has changed a lot since then, but I think one thing remains the same. Moms will never get enough credit for all the work they do.

> *She speaks with kindness, guiding people in God's truth.*
> *— Proverbs 31:26*

Ten Thoughts to Ponder

1. We can be thankful for problems, for without them, we might not recognize our need to be closer to the Lord.
2. Heaven is such a great place that people are dying to get there.
3. Judas's betrayal began with using Jesus to further his selfish desires, long before he saw Temple leaders or kissed Jesus at Gethsemane.
4. The stain of sin doesn't bother the Lord, because he has the perfect spot remover.
5. Like parents who love all their children, God loves each of us in a unique, unconditional way in which we must be treated differently.
6. Since God is everywhere, he can be found anywhere, but only if we're looking.
7. We trust technology, even though it doesn't always work. We should always trust the Lord, because he is forever at work in the best possible way.
8. Artificial flowers look more alive than dried flowers, but both are dead, incapable of growth.
9. Without God's direction, we are victims of our thoughts and desires that will lead us another way.
10. Salvation with its immediate transformation is a lifelong process.

Questions for Further Thought

- What are the best ways for children to honor their parents?
- Why might a mother's faith sometimes be ignored?

Unbearable Truth

After Samuel Shenton established the Flat Earth Society in 1971, he had to address the satellite images that showed Earth as a sphere. "It's easy to see," he said, "how a photograph like that could fool the untrained eye."

Denying the truth is easy. We simply embrace something else. Therefore, we need God's help with the truth we struggle to believe.

> *I have much more to tell you, but you cannot handle it right now. But when the Spirit of Truth comes, he will guide you into all truth.*
> *— John 16:12–13*

Ten Thoughts to Ponder

1. Asking lots of questions is a wonderful way to keep the door open to hearing God's answers.
2. We can always do what is, to best of their knowledge, most pleasing to be Lord—and with that desire, the Holy Spirit will help us do even better.
3. The past is not changeable, but with God's help, it is either forgettable or memorable.
4. Since I can't use tools I don't have, I'm compelled do my best with God's help.
5. We might as well accept the simplicity of God's grace, because the complexity is far beyond our ability to understand.
6. The truth will set us free, but only if we hear, believe, and do God's will.
7. Freedom from Egypt meant nothing to the Israelites if they could not be free from their idolatry.
8. Of all the things we might say, only one message is most right.
9. Like some greedy Christians, Judas used Jesus for self-gratification and never learned the value of self-sacrifice to help others.
10. The Lord may not come when we think, but he will be on time.

Questions for Further Thought

- How can we know when to accept or reject an apparent truth?
- How can our need for evidence balance our need for faith?

Selfies

Ages ago, photographers set a camera's timer and ran to be included in the picture. Now, we just snap a selfie on our cellphones.

One day, I'll be the person God wants me to be, and I'll take a perfect selfie.

> *When we look in a mirror, we see an imperfect reflection of who we are, but when we see the Lord face-to-face, we will see ourselves as he sees us.*
> — *1 Corinthians 13:12*

Ten Thoughts to Ponder

1. When we find ways to be active in God's will to help others, we are most valuable in his sight.
2. Since we can't walk through the filth of this world without getting dirty, we are in constant need of God's cleansing.
3. We will be in the likeness of Jesus because he is the perfect image of God in human flesh.
4. The difference between the exclamation mark and the question mark is *definitely knowing* or *just wanting* to know.
5. God became the Son of Man so we could become sons and daughters of God.
6. When hurting, we should first consult our Great Physician to see what prescription he might have for us.
7. With true faith, we can trust God in our trials, knowing that triumph is sure to follow.
8. When our problems appear to be too big for God, we should check to see if our binoculars are turned backward.
9. We need God's presence to guide us, or his Instruction Book won't make much sense.
10. Trusting God can be difficult, because from the beginning, Satan and his supporters have argued that God can't be trusted.

Questions for Further Thought

- How might personal insecurities and past experiences shape the way we see ourselves?
- How should God's unconditional love affect our self-image?

Servant Kingdom

A *king*-dom is ruled by a king—a monarchy, not a democracy or republic in which the people have a voice in government.

Jesus is no ordinary king. He's the King of kings and the Lord of lords, above all other authorities and powers. Yet he is the greatest of all servants, proved by the sacrifice of his life for our sake.

> *Christ died so we can live forever with him. A much better servant than God's messengers, he has earned a name above all others.*
> — *1 Thessalonians 5:10; Hebrews 1:4*

Ten Thoughts to Ponder

1. Apart from the Lord, anxiety and depression are unavoidable, for he is our security, and no other insurance is good enough.
2. Satan and his supporters do their best to convince us that sin is beneficial.
3. Jesus is our perfect example of the kind of people we are when we're completely committed to the direction of the Holy Spirit.
4. Salvation provides the means to be completely free from sin—if that's what we want.
5. Throughout human history, our spirit nature has been able to sense God's presence and learn what most pleases him.
6. In Christ, hope is anticipation of the good that God will surely do, not just wishful thinking.
7. If Christians value God's gifts more than their relationship with the giver, they need deliverance from idolatry.
8. With God, it's possible for us to rest while awake and work while we sleep.
9. To be good *listeners*, we must avoid focusing on speaking our minds or thinking about what we need to say next.
10. Preaching is an imposition that can make hearing the message difficult, but stories are music to our eager ears.

Questions for Further Thought

- How does Kingdom service differ from doing good things?
- What about helping others can be a perfect source of joy and satisfaction?

Kingdom Warfare

In God's Kingdom we have battles, but not with guns, tanks, and bombs. We wield different swords in spiritual warfare, not physical.

We struggle with forces that influence our desires, including social prejudices and leaders who promote what people want to hear and do.

"My Kingdom is not of this world," Jesus said. "If it were, my disciples would have fought to prevent my arrest by the Jews."
— John 18:36

Ten Thoughts to Ponder

1. Those who don't know God can think he doesn't love them or even exist.
2. In searching for life's meaning, we should ask the One who knows the most about us.
3. We can't say, "The devil made me do it," because from the beginning, God put enmity between our satanic, sinful nature and our godlike nature, so we make the choice.
4. God's invitation to Heaven comes with the required robe of righteousness.
5. When we are captured by the Lord, our surrender to do his will changes the nature of our battles.
6. We can't fully appreciate God's gifts until we have used them to fulfill his purpose.
7. God's glory shining through us explains why people can see our good works and glorify him, not us.
8. Unless the Lord guides my thoughts, I don't know what to think.
9. Without the Holy Spirit as our guide, we can be confused as we look at the obvious and cannot understand.
10. For people to see our good side, we need God's presence working through us.

Questions for Further Thought

- In what ways can worship and praise be considered spiritual weapons?
- How can we encourage people to stand firm in faith when they are facing trying times?

Father's Day

I was blessed with a father who gave me what I needed, not always what I wanted. This included spankings—an unavoidable consequence of my misbehavior. Of all my father gave me, my most valued possession is his love for God and people, which has grown in me.

Bad as you are, you know how to give good gifts to your children. How much more will your heavenly Father give only what is good to those who ask him.
— *Matthew 7:11*

Ten Thoughts to Ponder
1. What we call detours can actually be God's redirection.
2. Walking with the Lord is always good. That relationship is crucial, or what people call "good" wouldn't be good at all.
3. In the face of God's power, Satan has no power, and his underlings have no power, either.
4. Joy in the morning is a choice we have in Christ, which is much better than choosing grumpiness.
5. As we pursue God, we're helped by knowing there will be rewards along the way.
6. The wonderful thing about temptation is choosing what is good and shunning what is evil.
7. If the Holy Spirit will guide me, I can abandon my ignorance and know what to do.
8. God considered the exorbitant cost of saving us and decided it was worth the sacrifice, even if many refused his gift.
9. We should praise the Lord at all times so the rocks, hills, and mountains don't have to.
10. Small things seem so trivial until we see the great consequence, such as temptation that so easily slips in through a wandering mind.

Questions for Further Thought
- Why might a father's time and presence be one of the greatest gifts he can give?
- How can a father's leadership help or hinder the spiritual growth of his children?

Price of Security

The man showed me his $500 bill with the face of President William McKinley. "I carry it," he said, "in case of an emergency."

I thought his $500 bill wasn't worth much, because he had no intention of spending it. If we think money is our security, we should think again, because it is so easily lost.

> *Do not store up treasure for yourselves on Earth, where moths and rust can eat it up and thieves break in and steal.*
> *— Matthew 6:19*

Ten Thoughts to Ponder
1. Walking on water, Peter feared the same wind and waves that Jesus walked through when Peter took Jesus' hand.
2. Since human logic tends to be illogical at times, we really need God's truth and direction.
3. If we wonder why we live in such a dark world, we should know that our light shines most brightly there.
4. We can keep saying we need God's help, because *everywhere* we go, we need his help.
5. If we delight in the Lord, we have his guidance, and with greater guidance, we delight in him even more.
6. In our ignorance, our speculations are easily perceived as fact—unless the Holy Spirit guides us to the truth.
7. Loving our enemies is impossible without the enablement of God's nature within.
8. Because we cannot do the work ourselves, we must be patient, trusting God for the work we cannot do, while we do all that we can do.
9. For *empowerment* to really have power, God's power must be linked to our total surrender.
10. If our perspective is right, we still need to understand the different perspectives of others so we can know how to help them know what is right.

Questions for Further Thought
- How can we feel secure when our future is so unpredictable?
- Why might the rich feel more insecure than the poor?

Worth the Cost

When I was a kid, I never saw a credit card. You couldn't buy anything if you didn't have the money or could arrange a loan with payments.

Our relationship with Christ can't be bought on credit, and there is no payment plan. But is it worth the cost of everything we have? That would depend on how much we value the relationship.

> *A poor widow put in two copper coins that were worth next to nothing. Jesus said, "The truth is, the poor widow has given more than all the others."*
> — *Luke 21:2–3*

Ten Thoughts to Ponder
1. Leading people to Christ and seeing the Holy Spirit transform lives from the inside out to fulfill God's purpose is much greater than the physical signs that Jesus did.
2. Jesus said he was the way, truth, and life, because without him, we have none of that.
3. After feeding a multitude with a few loaves and fish, changing the weather with a command, and bringing a dead man back to life with a single touch, he said his disciples would do more.
4. Delight is something we most need when we are lost in de darkness.
5. God keeps his promises, but in ways we might least expect.
6. If we are to love others as God does, including our enemies, our personalities must transform to be like him.
7. Pain turns to pleasure-filled praise when we have faith to see God's plan and purpose in it.
8. Since God is everywhere, finding him has to be easy—if we *really* want to find him.
9. God defines love beyond our capacity to fully understand—until the day when we get to meet him face-to-face.
10. The wicked are blessed by the presence of the righteous—until Judgment Day.

Questions for Further Thought
- What do you think is most difficult for people to give up?
- Why would people give up everything to follow Christ?

Life-or-Death Choice

In the beginning, Adam and Eve were in the likeness of God, but that changed when they chose their own way. Our self-serving nature alienates us from him, but he gave us a choice to become like him.

Christ died for us. Now, the only question is whether we will die for him or die for something else.

> *You must make a choice ... As for me and my house, we will serve the Lord.*
> *— Joshua 24:15*

Ten Thoughts to Ponder

1. More than Satan's threat, we should be concerned about people who appear to be so innocent and helpful when their message would take us the wrong way.
2. We can't save ourselves, but God will if we accept his will.
3. Temptation can range from no more than an easily passed test to a strong desire to go the wrong way, but in either case, we need God's help.
4. The sheep belonging to the Good Shepherd come in all shapes, colors, and sizes.
5. Thinking *I should have what God had done for others* is too short-sighted, missing the different plan of glory that he has for us.
6. Being sent by God for even the smallest task is a tragedy if we don't accept the call.
7. When plagued by nightmares of feeling lost, alone, and incapable, we need God's presence to bring light upon our path and show us the way.
8. When God cries with us, we have the ultimate comfort in the midst of our pain.
9. The walk of faith is dangerous, possibly even fatal, when it trusts anything other than the power of the Holy Spirit to do what we cannot do.
10. When God touches our hearts, the miracle is just beginning.

Questions for Further Thought

- Why do people sometimes struggle to obey God?
- How can we increase our desire to please the Lord?

The Real Thing

Although cubic zirconia gems look the same, people pay a lot more for cut and polished diamonds from rocks dug from the earth. In a similar way, religious form is an unacceptable substitute for a relationship with Jesus Christ.

If we want the real deal, we must recognize the value and be willing to pay the price.

> *The Kingdom of Heaven is like a merchant seeking costly pearls. When he found one pearl of exceptional value, he sold everything he owned and bought it.*
> *— Matthew 13:45-46 Book #:#–#*

Ten Thoughts to Ponder

1. Jesus couldn't carry his own cross, because we must also bear his cross of surrender to live forever in his resurrection life.
2. If we always want his presence, God will walk with us for all the miles ahead, not just one.
3. Jesus gave us a behavior standard that is more demanding than the Law—impossible to do without a change of heart.
4. When God is our employer, we don't have to worry about our paychecks.
5. We could surrender more of our lives to the Lord if he would shine his light to reveal more of what needs to be surrendered.
6. Christians can celebrate victory before they see it, because it's guaranteed.
7. If we fail to practice what we preach, we can be sure we've been lying to ourselves and need an infusion of God's truth.
8. God can pull us up by the roots and plant us where he wants, but only if we're willing.
9. God delights in changing what we are helpless to change.
10. We may not fully comprehend God's love, but we should die trying.

Questions for Further Thought

- How can we distinguish between what is truly authentic or merely a very good imitation?
- How can we guard against false teaching but be open to truth?

Pandering Prophets

Be a master at telling people what they want to hear, and they'll believe you, even if what you say isn't true. They might even call you a prophet or "God's special messenger."

We don't have to be pandering prophets to have friends and influence people. All we must do is show genuine care. Some will appreciate hearing the truth, even if it hurts.

> *Woe to the politically correct, those who say what people want to hear, for that is what their fathers liked about the false prophets.*
> *— Luke 6:26*

Ten Thoughts to Ponder

1. Concern for the prize should focus on the process, which should focus on the next right step, which should look for the next thought that is the mind of Christ.
2. What Jesus paid makes us priceless treasures.
3. For complete surrender to the Father's will, Jesus needed *three* prayers in the garden of Gethsemane, not just one.
4. Chains remind us of our need for God's deliverance.
5. Anticipation of God's goodness is misplaced when we, like Jonah, have chosen to go our own way.
6. We need the Lord's help to find the bright side of the dark side.
7. When I don't know, I must proceed with the ignorance of what I don't know, hoping that the Lord will somehow help my ignorance.
8. We bless the name of Jesus by doing what he wants.
9. God's strength, power, and knowledge builds upon everything in the past so we can have something better in the future.
10. If we want to follow the way to eternal life with Christ, we must abandon the way of the world.

Questions for Further Thought

- How can we recognize the difference between a true prophet of God and someone who only says what is popular?
- Why do people often prefer to listen to messages that make them feel good rather than the truth?

Called by Name

One day, I asked my four-year-old friend what his father's name was. "Daddy." I asked what his first and last name were, thinking I would learn what his given first name. "Daddy Cox," he said, "like me."

More than anything, I'd like to be known as a child of my heavenly Father, with a name that clearly identifies me as part of his family.

> *Instead of coming in royal attire, asking to be served, he worked as a lowly member of the servant class. As an ordinary human being, he subjected himself to death on the cross. Therefore, God has promoted Christ to the highest of all positions and has made the name Jesus greater than any other name.*
> *— Philippians 2:7–9*

Ten Thoughts to Ponder

1. With five loaves and two fish, Jesus created something out of nothing, and that is really something.
2. Jesus' love for us is the expression of the Father's love that we can understand.
3. As Peter tried to walk on water, he learned that Jesus could help him more than he could help himself.
4. To sense God's presence and see his miraculous work, believing must precede seeing.
5. With God, one size doesn't fit everybody, but he has the perfect fit for our unique size and shape.
6. The most crucial part of God's direction is simple: We only need to know the next step.
7. What I most need to understand is that I do not understand my needs as well as God understands them.
8. An unused tool might as well be a nonexistent tool, so we do well to be used of God.
9. If we keep swinging the bat, odds for hits get better.
10. Jesus' model prayer calls for God's will on Earth as in Heaven—because it's possible.

Questions for Further Thought

- In what ways can names influence our perception of others?
- How might nicknames be helpful or damaging?

Mulligans

The golfer looked steamed. "I'm out of mulligans," he said after three-putting the seventh hole. With enough mulligans, mediocre players can score like pros. We should be thankful for a forgiving God who allows mulligans when we make bad choices. When he says, "That shot doesn't count," we can learn from our mistake and strive to do better.

If we confess our wrongdoing, he is sure to forgive us and cleanse us from all unrighteousness.
— 1 John 1:9

Ten Thoughts to Ponder
1. As we walk hand-in-hand with the Lord, the wonderful benefit is having no need to fear.
2. If we cannot accept God's truth about reality, then we are bound by a lie while thinking we are embracing the truth.
3. Sometimes, we need to hear God's voice in our own words and practice what we preach.
4. Part of listening to the Lord is saying and doing, but we must be careful, being sure we have first listened well, or the saying and doing will not be right.
5. Life can be a thrilling roller coaster ride with unpredictable ups and downs, twists and turns—if the Lord rides with us.
6. As the Lord helps us with all the small things, tackling the big things becomes much easier.
7. More than simply being creative, our Creator is our Supreme Inventor, because everything he does is to satisfy a need.
8. We need God's direction to know when to pick up the pen and when to pick up the phone.
9. We must do God's will, fulfilling his purpose, or we have spent our lives on nothing that will last.
10. A spiritual letdown comes from a temporary disconnection from the power source.

Questions for Further Thought
- Why does God give second chances?
- What obstacles keep people from accepting the second chances that God offers?

Finding Love

I was just two years old, but I'll never forget the vacation when I first saw the stone faces on Mount Rushmore. That night in the motel room, I cried uncontrollably, homesick because I thought we'd left God behind, at the church next door to the parsonage where we lived.

Our desire to be loved can leave us dying of thirst in a desert of the stone-faced who don't really care—unless we know God is with us.

> *I will ask the Father, and he will give you another Guide, one who will always be with you, the Spirit of Truth. The world cannot receive him, because it neither sees him nor knows who he is. But you know, because he lives with you and shall be in you.*
> *— John 14:16–17*

Ten Thoughts to Ponder

1. Concern for the right thing helps us not to worry about the wrong thing.
2. Artificial light is nowhere close to being as life-giving as the Son light that shines upon us, day and night.
3. We never have to say goodbye to the Lord, because he can be our friend forever.
4. Instead of looking for God's presence at church, we should have his presence within us, everywhere we go.
5. Misguided strength is a tragic weakness that needs God's overcoming power.
6. God gives burdens too heavy for us to bear so we can experience his mountain-moving miraculous power.
7. We should be looking for what is *real*, not *religious*—the *faith*, not the *form*.
8. We need to worry about the right things, not the wrong.
9. Rocking chairs provide lots of movement and pleasant thrills, but they won't take you anywhere.
10. The graves of the righteous are empty because of Jesus' resurrection life.

Questions for Further Thought

- Why is the need to be loved so deeply rooted in our nature?
- In what ways do people seek love, good and bad?

Perfection

As a youngster growing up, I thought anything less than a perfect test score said I was a failure. Not good enough. That changed when I learned that God would be pleased with my best effort, regardless, and he would take care of the results.

If we can understand that neither people nor God expect us to be perfect, doing our best will be good enough. And we can always do that much.

> *I've not yet achieved the relationship that Jesus had with the Father when he walked on Earth, but I'm moving in that direction. I'm not yet perfect, but I strive to lay hold of that for which Christ Jesus laid hold of me.*
> — Philippians 3:12

Ten Thoughts to Ponder

1. As God's captive, we have his perfect guidance in our complete compliance to his perfect will.
2. If we're looking for God's touch, we should be ready for his transformation.
3. Our Lord who calmed the wind and waves does a greater miracle when he speaks to the turmoil in our hearts.
4. When everything is going wrong, it's time to give it all to the Lord who makes everything right.
5. The story can't end until God finishes what he started.
6. Jesus gave his greatest prayer in Scripture when he said, "Your will, not mine," and embraced his suffering at the cross.
7. When we think there is no hope, God is still the master of reversals.
8. Spiritual birth is only the beginning of God's transformation process to make us holy as he is holy.
9. Praise is nothing without heartfelt meaning behind the words.
10. The really dumb cow thinks the grass is greener on the other side of the fence, the one place where she cannot be.

Questions for Further Thought

- How can perfectionism affect creativity and productivity?
- In what ways can perfectionism affect our self-esteem?

Murphy's Law

Supposedly, whatever can go wrong will go wrong. Wouldn't it be nice if everything that went wrong would actually wind up right? It can.

One day, we will see the fulfillment of God's plan and will be reassured of his love. Why? Because God's Law trumps Murphy's Law.

All those who love God and are working to fulfill his purpose should know that all things will work together for good.
— *Romans 8:28*

Ten Thoughts to Ponder

1. For a face-to-face meeting with God, we need only to see Jesus.
2. To experience God's glory, we glorify him by doing the work he has called us to do.
3. When I'm running through a downpour, the umbrella that I left at home is worthless.
4. Satan is really dumb to think he can outsmart God, and we'd be even dumber to think he can.
5. God is our greatest creativity resource, because he created something out of nothing.
6. Choices may be permissible, acceptable, or preferable—but we need God's guidance to know for certain which one of all the good choices is the one most pleasing to him.
7. We should remind ourselves that Jesus is coming soon—because it could be today.
8. Unforgettable days may be memorable because we never want to see them repeated. Others are remembered because we would love to see them again.
9. I experience addition by subtraction by eliminating a negative influence for a positive effect.
10. Without God's help, we cannot possibly do all that he has called us to do.

Questions for Further Thought

- What role does faith play in how we respond to the idea of inevitable failure?
- How might Murphy's Law help or hinder preparation?

Just Ask

Sometimes I hear Christians say, "We have not because we ask not." However, the context of James 4:2 suggests this might not be a good thing, our self-serving desires being a source of strife in the church.

Jesus said the Lord would take care of what we need, even if we don't ask.

> *If God clothes the wildflowers that are here now and gone tomorrow, don't you suppose he will care for you? Seek first his Kingdom and his righteousness, and he will give you everything you need.*
> — Matthew 6:30, 33

Ten Thoughts to Ponder

1. Sometimes, we have multiple-choice opportunities, and the best answer is "none of the above."
2. If we embrace the always-present Spirit of God, we make ourselves participants in whatever miracle he chooses to do.
3. My strength is a weakness when I think I can do something independent from the Lord's will.
4. To determine how many people have a different perspective from yours, count the number of people present.
5. God's detours are important when they take us to where he wants us to be.
6. Eating the body and drinking the blood of Christ should be an infusion of his presence that makes us more like him, full of love and without sin.
7. The lowest seat at Jesus' table is better than the highest at any other.
8. What we do won't earn our salvation, but it makes all the difference in how we grow our relationship with the Lord.
9. With his cross, Jesus built a bridge to Heaven for us to cross.
10. If Jesus needed to customarily isolate himself for prayer, we can be sure we should customarily do that too.

Questions for Further Thought

- Why might people hesitate to ask for what they truly want?
- Can asking for what we want be seen as selfish, or is it a form of healthy communication? Why?

Nowhere to Hide

When children play hide-and-seek, the fun would be lost if they were never found. We would hide from our enemies, if we could, but we would never hide from our friends.

If God is our friend, we can walk with him hand-in-hand wherever we go. But if he is an enemy, someone to fear, there is no place to hide.

> *Where could I go and not find your Spirit there? Is there anywhere I could escape your presence? If I go to the farthest region of space and beyond, you are there. If I am laid to rest in the deepest grave, you are there.*
> — Psalm 139:7–8

Ten Thoughts to Ponder

1. When our personal concerns aren't God's concerns, we should be concerned.
2. From God's perspective, knowing all things past, present, and future, he must know what he is going to do before he does it, as if he is already done it. That truth is mind-boggling.
3. Our most difficult battles are those we wage within ourselves.
4. Our imaginations are creative enough for us to live in religious fantasies that are far removed from the physical and spiritual reality of God's creation.
5. To support what we want to be true, our desires will embrace a fantasy while we ignore the facts.
6. Until we surrender to his guidance, God lacks the power to force his perfect will into all we say and do.
7. The Creator of the Universe has enough energy left to give us the strength to do his will.
8. Jesus' divine nature led him always to obey his Father's will, the undeniable evidence coming through what he suffered.
9. After being burned, we learn to be cautious, not so curious.
10. After seeing and believing what God can do, apart from his revelation and guidance, we still can't be sure what he will do, for his thoughts are far above ours.

Questions for Further Thought

- Why do people try to hide from God?
- How can being fully known be both scary and liberating?

White Lies

People tell white lies when the truth would hurt. Saying what we really think might get us unfriended, so we twist the truth as a social courtesy. Doctors may slant their prognosis toward what the patient wants to hear.

A white lie turns black as soon as someone suspects we've not told the truth. But if we tell the whole truth and nothing but the truth, we can live with the most honest person we've ever known—ourselves.

If bitterness or jealousy rises in your hearts, don't be deceived. A competitive spirit based on greed, self-justification, and boasting will miss the truth.
—James 3:14

Ten Thoughts to Ponder
1. All that God has planned for us will take all of eternity.
2. A spiritual connection will affect the emotions and will also affect us physically, so we really need that connection to be with God and not some other spirit.
3. Turning the other cheek is a sign of great strength.
4. Standing on God's promises becomes security when we understand and accept his conditions of total surrender.
5. In the next thousand years, we'll be awestruck at what living and working with Jesus is like.
6. To learn from the Lord, he needs more than our presence. He needs us to pay attention, listen, and then do.
7. God can do more than save the day. He makes new days better than anything before.
8. When we can't see the way, God is our light to show us the next right step, and that's all we must know.
9. Great faith believes when there is no apparent reason.
10. For as long as we have a reason to fear an imagined threat, we are facing an undefeatable enemy.

Questions for Further Thought
- What do you think qualifies as a "white lie"?
- Is honesty always the best policy? Why?

Prayer Believing

Some think prayer doesn't matter, because God will do what he wants, anyway. Others pray and nothing happens, so they assume God either doesn't care, or he isn't listening. Actually, God has a plan.

The devils believe and tremble, so believing must be more than knowing the truth. Faith has the added dimensions of trusting God and surrendering to his will, which the evil spirits will not do.

> *We don't always know the Lord's will and what to pray for, but the Spirit prays through us with groaning that English words cannot express.*
> — Romans 8:26

Ten Thoughts to Ponder
1. Complete surrender to the Lord in the process leads to perfection as the prize.
2. People seek satisfaction even when they don't know what their needs are. Therefore, God's guidance is crucial because he knows our needs better than anyone.
3. Temptation isn't noticeable when we're already equipped to pass the test without hesitation.
4. While I waste my time wishing, I'm not doing much. While I'm busy about doing, I'm not wasting much time wishing.
5. God's guidance is crucial because we can't always see what's coming ... but he can.
6. People fail to practice what they preach, because preaching is easy, but the time, effort, and expense of doing is tough.
7. With moments of silence, spoken words have greater impact.
8. We are obviously not driven by some kind of computer program, because each of us have to work out our own salvation—with fear and trembling.
9. We should appreciate whatever God chooses to do, because that's our best choice.
10. We have countless reasons to trust God, but when we're not recognizing any reason, we face our greatest need to trust him.

Questions for Further Thought
- How can we guard against the prayer liturgy without faith?
- What does it mean to truly believe when we pray?

Unconvinced

Some say, "People convinced against their will are of the same opinion still." Courteous, people may nod as if they agree when they don't.

Tell people their beliefs are wrong, and they'll be defensive, no longer listening. People learn best by discovering answers themselves.

> *Be gracious with your stories, flavoring your message with that which will answer the hunger in everyone's heart.*
> *— Colossians 4:6*

Ten Thoughts to Ponder

1. A thought written is a thought preserved, which is otherwise soon forgotten.
2. We need to hear God, for one of the worst things that can happen is thinking we have answers when we really don't.
3. The Law shows our wrongs so Grace can lead us in all that is right.
4. We can forever bask in the joy that we get to live and move and have our being in intimate fellowship with the Lord.
5. Since God always keeps his Word, our concern should focus on whether we will keep ours.
6. Artificial Intelligence will either bite or benefit us, depending on how we choose to use the tools.
7. Job would be first to point out that God is the genius, and we're not that smart.
8. As soon as our goal seems unworthy of the price required to get there, we are ready to give up—unless our faith gives us reason to keep pressing on.
9. Without Jesus' direction and authority, using his name has no power.
10. When an impossibility is part of God's plan, impossibility becomes a possibility, which might become a probability or even a guarantee.

Questions for Further Thought

- Why do people struggle to believe the truth after hearing it?
- How can we help others who have heard the truth but aren't ready to believe it?

Good Investment

High-risk investments are made with hope for a greater reward. If we forgive an offense, what will we get in return? Maybe nothing. Or maybe the life we save will be our own.

When we forgive others, we can be forgiven for our own offenses.

If you forgive others for the wrongs they have done, your heavenly Father will forgive you. But if you refuse ... he will not forgive you.
— *Matthew 6:14–15*

Ten Thoughts to Ponder

1. We can more easily trust God when our commitment to his will says he can trust us.
2. Asking "why" questions makes God accountable to us, but asking "what" questions makes us accountable to him.
3. To say what the Lord would have us say, we must avoid saying what he doesn't want us to say.
4. Our relentless desire for achievement is misdirected unless we have a sense of God's purpose in what we are doing.
5. God's presence is his gift to us, because nothing and no one can satisfy our needs any better.
6. When we understand God the unconditional love and faithfulness of God, we can have complete confidence in his purpose for our lives.
7. Praising the Lord is best done now, not next weekend.
8. Asking God for something doesn't guarantee getting it, because he often has planned something better for us.
9. Use God's gifts today, because now is the best time to see their purpose fulfilled.
10. People often argue over the most trivial stuff while never noticing what really is important, which is one reason we should be desperate for God's guidance.

Questions for Further Thought

- How does forgiving someone reflect the heart and character of God?
- In what ways does forgiveness free the person doing the forgiving more than the one being forgiven?

Paying Gig

In 1950, while sitting atop the garage roof, I pulled another wood shingle from the bundle for Daddy to nail in place. For that simple task that lasted all morning, I was paid $2.00. Wow! I was rich.

Even at four years old, I was learning about the reward for my labor—which goes far beyond the value of money when we're working for the Lord.

> *Be strong in the Lord, passionate about doing his work, knowing that your effort will always have great value.*
> *— 1 Corinthians 15:58*

Ten Thoughts to Ponder

1. Standing on God's promises can be a challenge when we understand the costly conditions.
2. If God will give us clarity, we can know what to think or not to think, what to say or not to say, and what to do or not to do.
3. Truth is good. But understanding *why* it is true and *good* is much better.
4. I need more faith to see how I will express God's love to others in Heaven where there is no pain and suffering.
5. Knowing God is better than knowing ourselves, because he knows us better than we do.
6. God understands how my lack of understanding helps me understand my need to trust his understanding.
7. Praising the Lord is good. Knowing *why* we're praising him can be life-changing.
8. Saying, "I love you," is easy, but actually doing it, without just words, takes extra effort and some self-sacrifice.
9. The use of Jesus' name has power only if we use it under his direction and authority.
10. Singing, "Holy is the Lord," has value when we understand the meaning and magnitude of his holiness.

Questions for Further Thought

- What do you think "treasures in Heaven" look like?
- What motivates more, eternal reward or present results? Why?

Prayer to Be Blessed

Few people had ever heard of Jabez until *The Prayer of Jabez* book became a bestseller. Why was it so popular? For one thing, people loved the message that prayer could give them what they wanted.

What many people didn't understand was the motive behind the prayer. I think he was asking for more so he would have more to give.

Jabez prayed to the God of Israel, saying, "Bless me with great abundance. Make me highly successful. Be with me to prosper all my efforts. Save me from failure so I'll never be embarrassed."
God gave him what he asked for.
— 1 Chronicles 4:10

Ten Thoughts to Ponder

1. The invisible things in our lives are often the most consequential.
2. If we are not making progress in our own strength, we should recognize our weakness and look to the Lord who is our strength.
3. When the Lord is my driving force, motivation is good. Otherwise, I'm going the wrong way.
4. When what I say doesn't match what I do, I can be sure I'm lying to myself and need God's help to know the truth.
5. When we don't know the right questions to ask, God still has the right answers.
6. Whatever is most pleasing to the Lord should be most pleasing to us—if we choose to make it so.
7. Without God, our good deeds aren't very good.
8. I depend upon the Lord because I not only don't know what I don't know, but I don't know what I need to know.
9. Tests are short, but graduation is forever.
10. Without God's help, we cannot begin to imagine the realities of the spirit realm, either here or in Heaven.

Questions for Further Thought

- How can we know whether a request for blessing is driven by faith or by selfishness?
- Which of God's great blessings should we share with others?

Novice Story

Garrison Keillor once said we don't know how to tell a story until after we've told it a dozen times. Being a novice is normal.

In a few sentences, write how God changed your life. Practice that with your friends. After a dozen times, you'll know what approach works best to help strangers who need to hear your story.

[Jesus said,] "If anyone publicly acknowledges me before men, I will publicly acknowledge him before my Father in Heaven."
— Matthew 10:32

Ten Thoughts to Ponder
1. The best social connections are achieved by making ourselves captive to the Lord's will.
2. God cannot control our bad choices, or he would be guilty of causing evil, which is not in his nature.
3. When I'm doing nothing, I'm actually doing nothing except for one thing: nothing.
4. God makes no mistakes, because his perspective from outside time allows him to see the result before he begins his work.
5. Sin is a sweet pleasure until it turns sour.
6. To work out our own salvation with fear and trembling, we address the present concern, moment by moment, one day at a time.
7. When people called Jesus good, they were looking at the goodness of his flesh when they needed to see the generosity of his Spirit.
8. If we can't be honest with ourselves and with God, we are sure to live hypocritical lives of self-deception.
9. Some Christians look for *revival* when they need *resurrection*.
10. Jesus' baptism was a commitment to *ministry*. The transfiguration was a commitment to his *death*.

Questions for Further Thought
- What fears or insecurities do novices often face, and how can they be overcome?
- What role does vulnerability play in authentic telling of our life-changing stories?

Missteps

I've fallen down the stairs. Worse yet, I've fallen, going up the stairs. What special skill does that require? None. Just miss the step.

We fall by focusing on the goal and miscalculating the next step. Neither goal nor step is more important than walking with the Lord.

> *The steps of righteous people are directed by the Lord, and they love to walk with him. They may stumble, but they won't fall flat, because God will help them up.*
> — *Psalm 37:23–24*

Ten Thoughts to Ponder

1. Regret is a useless hindrance, because the only thing I can do with the past is learn from it and make the present better.
2. When we say we want to hear the Lord's voice, but we really don't, we will have a difficult time hearing what he would like to say to us.
3. Walking with the Lord works best when we're eager to go wherever he wants to go.
4. In the world, empowerment assigns a person skills to achieve something, but in the Kingdom of God, empowerment assigns his plan and power to our desire to do his will.
5. The bliss of ignorance is knowing I have a lot to learn.
6. With our complete surrender to God's will, temptation has no power to take us in another direction.
7. For people to live in darkness, they must avoid the light.
8. God's forgiveness loses its value if we keep sinning.
9. Faith allows us to walk in the light that our flesh cannot comprehend.
10. In the world, empowerment assigns a person skills to achieve something, but in the Kingdom of God, empowerment assigns his plan and power to our willingness to do his will.

Questions for Further Thought

- How can the voices we listen to—friends, media, culture—lead us toward or away from missteps?
- How do you balance *the need to take risks* with *avoiding missteps*?

Security

Saying, "Don't fear," doesn't calm the thoughts that torment us. When the wind and waves were about to capsize their boat, the disciples feared for their lives. Jesus said, "You of little faith, why are you so afraid?" They didn't recognize the value of having him in their boat.

When we recognize his presence and power, we don't have to fear.

Don't be afraid, for I am with you. Never be discouraged, because I am God, who will help you.
— Isaiah 41:10

Ten Thoughts to Ponder
1. Whatever God has in mind for us is better than what we would have in mind—unless what we have in mind is what he has in mind.
2. We pray because of a need. The more desperate the need, the more desperate the prayer.
3. With my good motives, I might think God's desire must match what I want, but the evidence suggests he might have something better in mind.
4. Salvation without transformation is a fantasy that will take people to Hell.
5. Prayers are always good, even when it's for something God either can't or won't do, because they bring us closer to him.
6. For some, church is a great place to feel good without having to change or do anything.
7. If people aren't walking hand-in-hand with the Lord, their relationship with him has little meaning.
8. Satan's skill as a liar comes from his ability to misapply and misdirect the truth.
9. If knowing Jesus is dawn's first glimpse of light, then sharing Jesus is the light of the midday Son.
10. Our best motivation for prayer should be to maintain closeness with God.

Questions for Further Thought
- In what ways do people try to find security outside of God?
- How does insecurity influence the choices people make?

Great Expectations

Fun would come right after church. Outside, looking up the steps, I threw my paper airplane into the air. Oh, no! I wanted to hide, but it was too late. It hit the lady coming out the door.

When we want to hide but can't, only one solution exists: Pray. Admit who we once were. Accept forgiveness. And take our spanking if necessary. After that, we can forget the past, because with God's help, we're becoming a new, better person.

If we confess our wrongdoing, he is sure to forgive us and cleanse us from all unrighteousness.
— 1 John 1:9

Ten Thoughts to Ponder

1. With forgiveness, past sins might be forgotten, but present sin will persist when we're not fully surrendered to God's will.
2. Being "born again" is the *beginning* of the salvation process, not the end.
3. People seek satisfaction everywhere, but the anticipated pleasure is never enough, increasing their dissatisfaction—until they find the Lord who truly satisfies.
4. Our life-changing stories will help *nobody* when *nobody* knows about them.
5. Without a good reason, we can be discouraged, but God has all the good reasons for us to be encouraged.
6. Walking with Jesus means we never have to feel alone.
7. Since Satan can roam and roar only where God allows, we should be most concerned about God's purpose, not Satan's.
8. Jesus is the way, truth, and life. Heaven has no backdoor entrance.
9. The gift of God's presence within is unusual, because instead of using his gift for our glory, the gift uses us for his glory.
10. Sharing is much easier when you don't feel threatened by the possibility you might be wrong.

Questions for Further Thought

- In what ways do expectations shape people's futures?
- How might lofty expectations lead to failure?

Fine Print

Before signing a contract, I must be sure I know what I'm agreeing to. Even a comma can change the meaning, so I may need a magnifying glass. I want a contract that works in my favor.

With God, if I read the fine print, I see that I must give up my life to save it. With that, I surrendered something worthless for eternal treasure.

> *What have you gained if you own the whole world but lose your life? Nothing has sufficient value that you should want to exchange it for your life.*
> — Matthew 16:26

Ten Thoughts to Ponder

1. With the use of AI, we should look for tools that help us do our work, but not for tools that will do all our work for us.
2. God works in our lives by invitation—by his, then ours.
3. Intelligence is knowing the fire is hot. Wisdom is knowing not to test and see how hot the fire is and be burned.
4. Prayer should be more about listening than about speaking.
5. Moses led people from Egyptian bondage to the Promised Land, but Jesus came to free us from sin so we could be with him forever—but only if we're willing.
6. When we hit rock bottom, we've found the perfect opportunity to stand on the Solid Rock.
7. All things working together for good is different for every individual, with a unique purpose for each of us.
8. If we can see the value, we will sacrifice our lives for the Lord's sake, and we won't if we don't.
9. The "prayer of faith" is total surrender to God's will, not intense believing he will give us what we want.
10. Sin is merely a symptom of misdirected desires that God would like to change.

Questions for Further Thought

- Why do people often skip over the fine print when signing contracts or agreements?
- How important is counting the cost before a commitment?

Lost Key

When I bought a van from a friend, I gave my single ignition key to my son so he could drive. That night, as we walked toward the house, he pitched the key back toward me. I felt it hit my hand, and I spent the next hour in vain, searching through the grass. Unbelievable. I found where the key had ricocheted into my pocket.

In searching, I must always have the Lord's help. Otherwise, I could spend the rest of my life searching but never finding.

> *"If you were blind," Jesus said, "you would be blameless. But because you say you can see, you remain blind."*
> *— John 9:41*

Ten Thoughts to Ponder
1. Without the application, which is doing what we know to do, having the right answers and guidance aren't much help.
2. Money given is better than money gotten.
3. When people don't know why our relationship with the Lord is worth dying for, we do well to show why that's true.
4. The best place to cry is on Jesus' shoulder, because nobody cares more.
5. We can beat ourselves down or lift ourselves up, but it's best to thank God for progress and keep looking for his help.
6. If we want to be effective and efficient, we should seek the Lord's help, for he's the best.
7. To do what God wants, we must be close enough to hear when he speaks, which is why we should pray a lot.
8. We will see Jesus in our lifetime, for he will either come to us on Earth or we will go to him.
9. If we are to be God's messenger, we are his voice, not merely a scribe who copies words given to somebody else.
10. Faith knows help is on the way when we can't see where or how the help is coming.

Questions for Further Thought
- What role does hope play in the search for something lost?
- How does recovering something lost change your appreciation for it?

Random Dots

When I look at the night sky, I see lots of stars, but I have trouble picking out the constellations. If only the stars had numbers. Then I could connect the truths and see the whole picture.

Sometimes I pray, "Lord, if you would number the dots, then I could see the whole picture."

> *He knows the number of stars in the sky and can call each one by name. Our Lord is great, with unlimited power and knowledge.*
> *— Psalm 147:4–5*

Ten Thoughts to Ponder
1. Since God knows and we know, we should know that we can't keep secrets from the two who matter most.
2. If we can't love our enemies, then we can't know how much Jesus loves us.
3. Walking with Jesus is a self-sacrificing choice, since we must be willing to surrender everything, even our lives.
4. Overcoming fear of tomorrow requires walking close to the Lord today.
5. Without a complete emotional surrender to God's will, our spirit is less willing, and the flesh will continue to fight for what it wants.
6. The day will come when God will uproot all that the Enemy has planted.
7. If we want to be overcomers, we need God working with us—or we might not be overcoming the right things.
8. God will spend as much time with us as we want.
9. We might not get to meet the president of the United States, but we can always walk with the King of kings and Lord of lords.
10. The size of the crowd doesn't always prove the depth of the messenger's conviction.

Questions for Further Thought
- Why is it easier to focus on a few details rather than the big picture?
- How can a limited perspective lead to poor choices?

Salvation

Ten dollars and reciting the Sinner's Prayer will buy a cup of coffee and a donut. It won't buy salvation, so I'm bothered when someone say, "If you said those simple words, you've been born again." Maybe.

I'm lying to myself when my actions don't match what I say. I think the great basis for salvation is found in the passionate words of Jesus as he prayed at Gethsemane before his suffering on the cross.

> *My Father, if you are willing, let me escape this suffering. Nevertheless, I want your will, not mine.*
> *— Luke 22:42*

Ten Thoughts to Ponder

1. To avoid wasting our time, we need God's guidance to know what he wants and what is not worth our curiosity.
2. We might not understand God, but we can still know him.
3. When we cling to our interpretations more tightly than to the Spirit of Truth, we risk becoming idolatrous blind guides like the Pharisees.
4. To make room for God-given desires, we sacrifice our self-serving desires.
5. Our works won't save us. Neither will our thinking too highly of ourselves. But we will be saved through our willingness to be led by the One who sees all things as they really are.
6. To surrender our problems into God's hands, we must let them go from our hands.
7. If we want others to be our friends, we must become friends to others, treating them like we would have them treat us.
8. Polishing an idol of doctrine is easier than carrying a cross of surrender.
9. Baptism is as much a commitment to our relationship with Christ as "till death do we part" in a marriage ceremony.
10. Restaurants on Mars is a bad idea. People wouldn't like the atmosphere.

Questions for Further Thought

- What does it mean to be saved?
- How should salvation affect the way we treat others?

Superhero

I'm not Superman. As soon as I imagine leaping over a building with a single bound, I see the kryptonite that says I lack sufficient strength. Superheroes aren't so super. Without God, I'd be a super failure. To achieve anything worthwhile, I need his guidance and his strength.

I know what it's like, both to abound and to suffer desperate needs. In all situations, no matter how little or how much I have, I must depend on Christ for my strength and guidance.
— Philippians 4:12–13

Ten Thoughts to Ponder

1. We should avoid going anywhere or even thinking anything without the feeling of God's presence.
2. Without faith, we have religious form, void of spiritual power.
3. Satan would tell us our mess-ups prove we have no hope, but faith knows God can cause it all to work for good.
4. Human comprehension of God is like an ant trying to understand an airplane.
5. I frantically fight the frustration and find myself even more frustrated—until I finally surrender my frustration to the Lord's control.
6. We do well to chase after God, because Jonah would say we don't want him chasing after us.
7. Seeing what isn't there is difficult, yet that might be the very thing we need to see—which is why we need God's vision.
8. If we strive to do God's will, he will work his miraculous results.
9. If we are close to the Lord, we can be comforted with the fact that God knows our thoughts, but otherwise, we should be concerned.
10. God is *Who*. *What* is relationship. *When* is now. *Why* is life. *How* is Jesus Christ.

Questions for Further Thought

- What makes someone a true hero?
- What qualities or choices set heroes apart from the average person, even when they have no special powers?

Legal Immigrant

Many jokes suggest requirement to pass the pearly gates and enter the Kingdom of Heaven. Jesus said it isn't enough to profess him as Lord. If I love him, I will surrender what I want so I can enjoy the blessing of doing what he wants. If I keep on sinning, I can't sneak in.

> *Your self-serving nature can lead you to such things as infidelity ... contentions, anger, and resentment ... Don't think for a second that you can do such things and have any place in the Kingdom of God.*
> — *Galatians 5:19–21*

Ten Thoughts to Ponder
1. When we are looking for God to do something, we should know that he already has, he already is, and he already will.
2. The highway to Heaven has a toll: surrender to the God's will.
3. Some people think being used is demeaning, but with God, the meaning of being used is to share in his glory.
4. Our worst days can turn out to be the greatest when we're walking with the Lord.
5. When so many coincidences line up for us not to believe they are coincidences, we can be sure we are experiencing more than mere coincidence.
6. When Satan thought Jesus was dead and buried, his gloating didn't last very long.
7. While complaining, wishing conditions were different, we cannot enjoy the value of embracing the way things are.
8. God can use our great messes to do unimaginable miracles.
9. Progress is having more of God's help to do more of all that needs to be done and less of all that needs not to be done.
10. God's voice to people's hearts can be understood in all languages.

Questions for Further Thought

- How do baptism, confession, and other outward expressions factor into the process of salvation, if at all?
- What evidence would prove that a person really does believe in his heart and confess with his mouth that Jesus is Lord?

Challenging Steps

I've never walked a tightrope. I was challenged to walk the top edge of a twelve-foot-long 2x10 that supported a homemade swing. As I approached the middle, the board began to sway. I lost my balance and took a flying leap eight feet to the ground.

Since my childhood days, I've learned to be more cautious. Now, I want the Lord walking with me. Always.

The Lord will help those who stumble and fall. He'll lift up those who have reached rock bottom.
— Psalm 145:14

Ten Thoughts to Ponder

1. If variety is the spice of life, we should be delighted to follow the Lord, who is unbelievably creative.
2. The more I try not to remember, the more impossible it is to forget.
3. Persistence says giving up is not an option. Patience says we need God's help if persistence is to take us in the right direction.
4. Thanksgiving and praise are good, but worship is the wonderful spiritual connection with God.
5. When walking with the Lord, we can know that all is well, although circumstances would say otherwise.
6. Without the need, there could be no miracles.
7. When Jesus said, "It is finished," he marked the end of one thing and the beginning of something much greater.
8. With our testimonies and wholehearted commitment to God's will, Satan is defeated.
9. When our predicament makes prayer a priority, we learn to trust the Lord and be thankful in all things.
10. Sceva's sons proved that using the name Jesus was worthless without the relationship.

Questions for Further Thought

- How should walking with the Lord affect our choices?
- What are some practical ways to stay close to God throughout a busy or challenging day?

God's Great Miracles

Wanting God's glory revealed in my life, I prayed to be a miracle. Oops! Suddenly, I realized how dangerous such a prayer was. For a miracle, I would have to suffer dire needs. I've had my share.

God's great miracle doesn't change how we look or what we have. We're a miracle because God has changed who we are. We're living a miracle, because he is still working within us to fulfill his purpose.

> *Like someone looking into a mirror, we see the beauty of who we will become, more and more like the Lord, being changed from glory to even greater glory by the work of his Spirit.*
> *— 2 Corinthians 3:18*

Ten Thoughts to Ponder

1. Our views of God can be correct, yet as different as three blind men describing an elephant as a tree, snake, or wall.
2. We cannot be tempted if we believe we have no choice.
3. Reading God's Word doesn't have the same benefit as hearing his voice, understanding his purpose, and sharing his message.
4. The stronger the conflict or dilemma, the more powerful and captivating our stories will be.
5. Easy victory lessens the value of the prize.
6. A well-told story is irresistible, which is why our testimonies should be stories.
7. When people don't want to do what they feel they should do, they will find an excuse that justifies their desire.
8. Worrying about what we can't control steals energy from what we can and should control.
9. Not knowing exactly where we're headed, we see the fulfillment of our purpose by following the Lord.
10. Accepting reality can be difficult when that isn't the way we want it to be.

Questions for Further Thought

- What are some easily overlooked miracles in everyday life?
- How should we respond when we pray for a miracle and don't receive what we asked?

One Essential Part

At two years old, I loved putting together picture puzzles.

Before God created any of his pieces, he had the complete picture in mind. In the end, when all his pieces come together, he'll enjoy a breathtakingly beautiful picture of his greatness and glory, in which we are one essential part.

> *All of you together make up the body of Christ, each of you being a unique, essential part.*
> *— 1 Corinthians 12:27*

Ten Thoughts to Ponder

1. With God's help, we can do anything—but we can't do everything, which is why we need God's help.
2. I want God to be my influence, because I see no need to influence God.
3. Since God wants to do with us something different from anybody else on Earth, we have no person to idolize, not anywhere on Earth.
4. Of all that matters on Earth, our relationship with the Lord matters most.
5. We don't have to worry about memory as long as we have the right thoughts for the present moment.
6. As we walk with the Lord, our stumbling blocks become steppingstones.
7. Even with what seems to be the perfect vision, people are sure to perish—unless they have God's vision.
8. We can easily create a very long word by eliminatingallthespacesbetweenwords.
9. Many people will leave their comfort zones to do God's will—as soon as they are made uncomfortable.
10. Disobedience becomes tempting when we imagine the benefit of going our own way.

Questions for Further Thought

- How does being part of the Body of Christ differ from attending church?
- How can Christians appreciate being different from others?

Hearing Aid

People sometimes say, "God never talks to me." That may have more to do with their hearing than with him speaking.

With his "still, small voice," I must listen carefully. I'm not sure I would listen any better if he were shouting. The tough part is having to accept what he has to say.

> *If you have an ear to hear, you should listen to what the Spirit is saying to the churches.*
> — Revelation 3:22

Ten Thoughts to Ponder

1. The present moment is most crucial because it gives meaning to the past and changes the future.
2. Accountability to God is most important, because with him, we can't get away with anything.
3. Looking for a problem's solution can be tough when we want God's answer and don't know where to look. So we pray a lot.
4. God helps those who help others, not those who help themselves.
5. When patience and productivity work together, we have sustainable progress with purpose.
6. I almost had a thought, and I thought I had lost my thought until I thought again.
7. God has the best form of anticipation possible, because he knows the out-come before the in-come.
8. Our pursuit of excellence can be worthless if it isn't focused on pleasing God.
9. I know what I know. Otherwise, I'm not sure whether I know. Either way, I could be wrong, which keeps me looking for what God knows.
10. Human nature is such that it can be overwhelmed with nothing to do.

Questions for Further Thought

- How is God's voice distinguished from our own thoughts?
- In what ways do Scripture, prayer, and circumstances work to help us discern God's guidance?

Talent Scout

I dreamed of who I could be—a doctor, a lawyer, a scientist. I might be any one of them, but I couldn't be all of them. Nobody ever suggested I should be a writer or speaker. Obviously, I had no talent there.

Talent is overrated, because God is the Great Enabler. Without his help, our accomplishments have little value.

> *When you are arrested, do not worry about what to say. Whenever you must speak, you will be given the right words to say. You will not be the one speaking. The Spirit of your Father will speak through you.*
> — *Matthew 10:19–20*

Ten Thoughts to Ponder

1. To have God on our side, we must abandon our self-serving ways to join his side of giving with extreme love and grace.
2. If we embrace rejections, they can be wonderful opportunities to learn, improve, and make new and better connections. But otherwise, they can destroy us.
3. The first step of progress is learning to want God's way above our way, no matter how great the cost.
4. Revival is good. Resurrection is better.
5. Wisdom is knowing when to speak and when to shut up, and for that kind of insight, we need God's help.
6. We shouldn't think God doesn't need us, for we were created to fulfill his purpose.
7. When the Lord, not our flesh, gives us the desires of our heart, we get to live his miracles, one step at a time.
8. If Jesus had to pray before taking his cross, we should too.
9. With each telling of our life-changing stories, we get to experience God's miracle one more time.
10. Waiting upon the Lord is to serve him, not waiting for him to serve us.

Questions for Further Thought

- How can belief that talent is "essential to success" discourage people from pursuing what God would have them do?
- What qualities or practices should we prioritize when trying to master a skill or succeed in a challenging field?

Doing Fine

I've been so focused on one thing that I missed something more important—like when my absentmindedness led to a speeding ticket. Or when I was so engrossed in my work that I missed my appointment.

I think I'm doing fine—until I find out I'm not.

> *While earning their master's degrees and doctoral credentials, making themselves appear wise, they become fools. God has given them free will to go their own way.*
> — Romans 1:22, 24

Ten Thoughts to Ponder

1. Every time we learn something new, we experience a small breakthrough—maybe something life-changing.
2. If we walk with the Lord, we never have to feel alone.
3. Saying the past dictates what God can do in the future is shortsighted, failing to see how God habitually does new things.
4. We should never let go of our dependence upon God, for that is our life.
5. Some things I know—but I don't know that I know. If I did know, then I would know more than what I now know.
6. If prayer without ceasing is good, praising God relentlessly must be spectacular beyond words.
7. We know we need God's help when we see our extreme ignorance and inability to fulfill what he has for us to do.
8. If we put the past behind us and don't worry about the future, we can do better with today.
9. Nothing is more devastating than to feel rejected by God—when acceptance is just a repentance away.
10. "I can do it" is a terrible confession when it weakens our dependence upon the Lord.

Questions for Further Thought

- What emotions or fears might be behind people saying they're fine when they really aren't?
- How might we help people open up when they insist they're fine but we suspect otherwise?

Conditional Promises

A little box on the dining room table contained colored cards with Bible promises of God's blessing. They were wonderful. I thought they were free until I learned about the conditions.

The Bible makes quite clear what I should expect if I choose not to follow him but decide to go my own way.

> *To experience God's promises, we must always say yes to him, just as Jesus did. For when we are in complete agreement with his purpose, we share his achievements and glory.*
> *— 2 Corinthians 1:20*

Ten Thoughts to Ponder

1. Religious beliefs and traditions are bondage, not freedom, when they keep us from seeing God's truth.
2. Before we are willing to pursue anything worthwhile, we must believe the reward will be worth the effort.
3. Since what I think is important is not always what God knows is important, I need his guidance to know what is important.
4. When God is the supplier of our needs, the more we give, the more we will have to give.
5. If we know the Lord well and remain close to him, we should know there is no possibility of failure.
6. Our profession of ignorance opens the door for us to acquire God's knowledge and wisdom.
7. If a leopard can't change his spots, we might think we can't change, but God has spot remover to bring us his glory.
8. With the Lord's help, we can do what people thought was impossible.
9. What I think is important really is most important—unless I am led to believe something else is more important.
10. The blood of the Lamb is much more important than green eggs and ham. Or so says Sam.

Questions for Further Thought

- How do Jesus' words—"If you love me, keep my commandments"—shape our understanding of obedience and promise?
- What obstacles do people face in receiving God's promises?

Road Builder

My toy cars and trucks weren't dune buggies for the beach, so I used most of the sand from my sandbox to build a road down our gravel driveway. With a steady, "Varoom ... varoom," I delivered each dump-truck load to pave the way for all the heavy traffic to follow.

Like when I was young, we should remove every obstacle and pave a road for people to follow the Lord freely and unhindered.

> *Let it be said, "Rebuild the road. Prepare the way. Remove the roadblocks that keep God's people from coming to him."*
> — Isaiah 57:14

Ten Thoughts to Ponder

1. In prayer believing, I can be thankful for two things: to tell God what I want and to always receive whatever God wants.
2. To make room for the Lord, I need to take out the trash.
3. The Lord let me go my own way so I would be convinced that my own way wasn't worthy of pursuit.
4. Peace during the battle comes from total confidence that the Lord will bring victory in whatever form and means he chooses.
5. By claiming something we don't have, as if we already have it, we risk faking it without ever making it.
6. Learn to enjoy work, and life can be a year-round vacation.
7. Frustration is useless, because it assumes responsibility for something we cannot control. If we could, we wouldn't be frustrated.
8. Trying is good, but asking for the Lord's help brings his success, which is better than trying.
9. For us to understand God's truth with certainty, the Holy Spirit must lead us past our religious traditions and misbeliefs that we have rigidly held as undeniable truth.
10. Misplaced hope is actually hopelessness masquerading as a promise that will never be fulfilled.

Questions for Further Thought

- What kinds of roadblocks keep people from following the Lord freely?
- How can we encourage people to the road to eternal life?

Perfect Plan

All the bankruptcies over the years have taught me to face reality. No matter how much faith I think I have, striving for success on my own terms can be wasted effort—because my plans are typically flawed.

The perfect plan will be fulfilled as I let go of self-serving ambitions and follow God's vision for my life.

> *Trust God with your whole being, and don't rely solely upon what you think is true. Let the Lord guide everything you do, and he will keep you on the right path.*
> *— Proverbs 3:5–6*

Ten Thoughts to Ponder

1. I think God can give me thoughts much better than anything I can think on my own. Or at least that's what I think I think.
2. The truth is believed by those who want to know the truth, and that's the sad truth.
3. The greatest impossibility we face is to be someone we're not, for we need God's help to become who we need to be.
4. We can believe prayer changes things if we can see the things that prayer changes.
5. In hearing God's voice, we have his Word that becomes the basis of faith that moves mountains.
6. The more we walk with the Lord, the better we can understand and embrace his vision.
7. I am helped by sharing my desires with the Lord, because then I can set them aside to have whatever he desires.
8. When we don't know where we're going, we need to trust the One who does.
9. Waiting seems to be a waste of time—unless we believe our waiting has value that justifies the time.
10. Our personal pursuit of God's will is crucial if we want to help others.

Questions for Further Thought

- Why might following God's vision be difficult?
- In what ways has your definition of "success" changed over time?

Christmas Treasure

Last Christmas, Johnny got a King James Bible with his name stamped in gold. He proudly carried it to church but never read it. This year, he tore away the wrapping and found a thick comic book with all the Bible stories. He read those stories so much that the cover fell off.

God's Word is a treasure—but only if we read it.

> *I rejoice in your instructions like someone who has found a great treasure.*
> *— Psalm 119:162*

Ten Thoughts to Ponder

1. We do well to admit our wrong perceptions so we can open our minds to hear from the Lord and know what is right.
2. If prayer without ceasing is good, relentless praise must be spectacular.
3. Sometimes we have a problem in thinking we do not have a problem, just because we can't see the problem.
4. Peace is not having to worry about the future—because we know God is in control.
5. God's presence is everywhere, but for him to be "with" us, we must make a conscious move toward him.
6. Faked optimism is a mask that fools no one for long, not even ourselves.
7. People gathered "in Jesus' name" are those who respect his authority and want to follow his guidance.
8. God is the greatest of all providers, responding to the needs we don't even know we have.
9. Not only is persuasion needed to convince others, but we also need to be persuaded ourselves—that God's way has the greatest of all rewards.
10. Our plans are a waste of time unless they are fulfilled under God's authority and direction.

Questions for Further Thought

- Why might people acknowledge the importance of Scripture but seldom read the Bible?
- What treasures will we miss if we don't read the Bible?

Positive Thinking

As a kid, I thought "later" meant "never." That wasn't always true, but that's the way I felt because I wanted to hear, "Yes, right now." Either way, I had to face reality. The answer was no, at least for a while.

When my positive thinking doesn't happen, I must redirect my thinking. God has a better plan. I need to be careful lest I do what is right in my own eyes. That kind of positive thinking can be fatal.

> *There is a way that seems right but ends in death.*
> *— Proverbs 14:12*

Ten Thoughts to Ponder

1. When people are "in the way," I'm not sure whether they are in the way of following Jesus or if they are in the way of blocking what God wants to do.
2. We should be thankful that God sees who we will be, not just who we've been or who we are.
3. Standing on God's promises means saying, "Yes, sir. Whatever you want, sir," being fully committed to his will.
4. At the Last Supper, Judas was closest to Jesus physically, yet the farthest away in his heart.
5. Looking back not only hinders forward progress, but it also invites accidents due to failure to see what is ahead.
6. We should feel wonderful about achieving our dreams—but only if we have pleased the Lord.
7. The truth is not established through argument, conviction, or agreement—but our acceptance of truth might be.
8. Our strength is in the Lord, or we make ourselves victims, not victors.
9. With our weakness, God can reveal his strength. With our ignorance, God can reveal his knowledge and wisdom.
10. Faith is hearing and believing God, not necessarily believing what we want to be true.

Questions for Further Thought

- What is the difference between faith and positive thinking?
- When does positive thinking cross the line into wishful thinking or unrealistic expectations?

Prison Bars

In the synagogue, when Jesus said he had come to set people free, I doubt that his audience saw themselves as captives.

Spiritual captivity hides behind the illusion of freedom. Therefore, our greatest miracle isn't breaking chains. It's finally seeing them.

> *The Spirit of the Lord is upon me because he has anointed me to preach good news to the poor. He has sent me to comfort the brokenhearted, proclaim liberty to the captives, freedom for the oppressed, and recovery of sight for the blind.*
> *— Luke 4:18*

Ten Thoughts to Ponder

1. If what we desperately want is the same as what God wants, we avoid becoming victims to any temptation to do otherwise.
2. A well-focused prayer desires to please God more than self.
3. Of all the things that we would like to have more, we have no greater need than to have more of whatever God wants to work in our lives.
4. A picture says more than words, but the right words create the perfect pictures.
5. If our desires match what God wants to do, then we have a powerful agreement that is sure to be fulfilled.
6. If I think I already know, I am in danger of missing the truth that I really need to know.
7. We should have an insatiable appetite for experiencing God, not just to embrace a promising description.
8. Following the Lord may seem without purpose, but we can be sure it's better than planning on our own.
9. I would rather be confused by the truth than be confident in what I thought was the truth but really wasn't.
10. Without God's insight, it's impossible to be sure everything will be all right.

Questions for Further Thought

- How can religious tradition mask spiritual captivity rather than reveal it?
- What makes it difficult to recognize ways we aren't truly free?

Good Works

People sometimes assume they'll be in Heaven if they are "basically good." Actually, our relationship with God through Christ brings eternal life and determines whether our works really are good.

Salvation is not about the goodness we see in ourselves but whether we know and follow the One who is good.

> *Many will say, "Lord, didn't we prophesy, cast out evil spirits, and do many wonderful deeds in your name?" Then I will tell them, "I never knew you. Get away from me, you disobedient lawbreakers."*
> — Matthew 7:22–23

Ten Thoughts to Ponder

1. Even in pain and suffering, people can fear change—afraid their future state would be worse than the present.
2. Adventure will ignore danger, but complacency will imagine danger that isn't there.
3. I was thinking about thinking and thinking how wonderful it is when God can guide my thinking.
4. A self-guided ship has virtually no chance of arriving at the appropriate dock.
5. The distinction in storing treasures in Heaven, not Earth, is in whether we value ministry above money.
6. Without quality, quantity might be nothing more than a mountain of trash.
7. At every moment of the day, I have the means to do whatever God wants—but only if it's what I want too.
8. People feel naked when they have something they need to hide.
9. Knowing what to do is good, but knowing how to do it is better. Actually doing God's will is the bestest.
10. Looking is easy, but if we want to be good at finding, we need God's help.

Questions for Further Thought

- What role do motives play in determining whether our works are good in God's sight?
- How can we know our works are pleasing to the Lord?

Apples and Oranges

Comparing myself to anyone else is foolish—like an apple looking at an orange and saying, "I'm better because I'm an apple" or "I'm worse because I'm not an orange." I might prefer apples over oranges, but that's without regard for the orange's unique purpose.

Our value depends on our fulfillment of God's purpose for our lives, not the opinion of others.

We dare not be like others who brag about what they say and do, ranking themselves by using themselves as a standard for greatness, which isn't very smart.
— 2 Corinthians 10:12

Ten Thoughts to Ponder
1. Increased knowledge and ability make it difficult to know which thing to do out of the multitude of things we could do.
2. Contentment is knowing we know and knowing that we really do know that we know.
3. Like the ladder that has only one top rung, there is only one best choice that is most pleasing to the Lord.
4. We should follow the bouncing ball—but only if it's God's ball and his bounce.
5. Readers are captivated when stories are so real that they must be true yet are so miraculous that we wonder how.
6. When the Lord is our guide, our concern can soon be replaced with confidence.
7. What God will do is difficult to predict, for he is always building something new upon what he has done before.
8. Perhaps God's *plan* seems like a painful process, but the *prize* makes it both profitable and necessary.
9. When Jesus said, "It is finished," he introduced a new age of Grace—profoundly better than life under the Law, yet more demanding.
10. An untested belief is just wishful thinking.

Questions for Further Thought
- Why might people need to compare themselves with others?
- How can we guard against making unwise comparisons?

Rose Gardens

If God promised a rose garden, he didn't take away the thorns. Like it or not, on Earth pain and suffering is unavoidable.

We keep going when we are weak, because he is strong. We keep trusting when we don't understand, because we know he's always faithful. We have hope because we know who holds the future, not because circumstances are easy, but because God is with us in the storm.

> *Troubles press us from every direction, but we aren't crushed. We may not know what to do, yet we're confident that everything will work out.*
> — *2 Corinthians 4:8*

Ten Thoughts to Ponder

1. Having the right tools is a waste if we don't know how to use them in the right place, in the right way, at the right time.
2. An u*nexpected* answer is still a *good* answer when it comes from the Lord.
3. If we can have more of God, which is our antidote for our ignorance, we can save ourselves from a lot of grief.
4. Greater than God's love given to us is his gift for us to love others.
5. Sticks and stones break bones, but words cut to the heart.
6. Since we can do *anything* but cannot do *everything*, we need God's help to choose the best thing.
7. Since there isn't enough time to research every possibility in all directions, we need help to know where to look.
8. We do better to cause trouble for the devil than to allow him to cause trouble for us.
9. If God will show us the way, we can distinguish the difference between detours and his direction.
10. Getting it right the first time is important, because it saves all the cost for making it right, later.

Questions for Further Thought

- How can pain draw us closer to God, rather than push us away?
- When everything feels broken or uncertain, what is hope like?

Cosmic Bellhop

If I think God is my Cosmic Bellhop, I should remember that Jesus said he'll lighten my load. He didn't say he'd carry all my bags for me.

With a Father who knows and supplies our needs all the time, we can rejoice. Being content with his provision, we can strive to do what is right, knowing he will give us strength. We don't need someone to carry all our bags for us.

> *Take my yoke upon you, and learn to walk my way, for I am gentle and humble of heart. In me, you will find rest for your souls, because my yoke fits and your share of the load is light.*
> — Matthew 11:29–30

Ten Thoughts to Ponder
1. The more we learn, the more we can be sure we don't know anything compared to what God knows.
2. Human nature can embrace sayings without knowing what they really say, let alone what they mean.
3. In searching for truth, our greatest need for discovery might be the existence and nature of our misbeliefs.
4. If Jesus is our model for who we are to become, we need to know him very well.
5. With God, perfection is a reality, not merely a dream.
6. Reading God's Word isn't the same as hearing his voice and sharing his vision.
7. The perfect peace that God provides through Jesus Christ cannot be adequately explained with English words.
8. We may not understand God's peace, but it sure is wonderful to experience it.
9. The best way to express our gratitude for his gifts is to use them wisely in fulfillment of his purpose to help others.
10. I think God's way is always the best, no matter what I think.

Questions for Further Thought

- How can we distinguish between trusting God and expecting him to do everything for us?
- What is the difference between legitimate responsibility and unnecessary burdens?

The Doctor Is In

When I was little and hurting, the doctor never asked what was wrong with me. How would I know? He took my temperature and asked how I felt. From the symptoms, he guessed the disease and prescribed what he *thought* would help.

Our Great Physician knows exactly why I'm hurting and what I need to be well. But if I'm not willing to take the medicine he prescribes, I can't eliminate the symptoms, let alone cure the disease.

> *Sin is failure to do the good you know you should do.*
> *— James 4:17*

Ten Thoughts to Ponder

1. God is our best resource to know the truth, because he has all the right answers and is eager to share them—if we really want to know.
2. If we know more about what God is doing, we can do better at what we need to be doing.
3. My lack of understanding is a necessary part of the learning process to become the person God wants me to be.
4. The presence of a thought can pressure my thoughts until I change my way of thinking.
5. We may not have all the answers, but we can take great comfort in knowing we know the One who does know.
6. What God knows is better than what we think.
7. No matter the cost, the truth is something I need to know, for that is where true satisfaction, peace, and liberty reside.
8. If at first you don't succeed … pray … and trust the Lord.
9. When I say, "I just believe the Bible," I might be rejecting truth for fear that it would disturb my comfortable misbeliefs.
10. The "evidence of God" is present for all to see, so nobody can truthfully say, "I didn't know."

Questions for Further Thought

- Why might it be difficult to recognize the real cause behind our struggles or suffering?
- How can we develop spiritual sensitivity to recognize when we're treating symptoms instead of addressing the root cause?

Most Wonderful Deal

I've noticed that most people will vote for *others* paying higher taxes. We want increased wages and lower prices. We prefer employers with great retirement plans, insurance, and time off with pay. Do you see a pattern here? We want the most we can get for the lowest cost.

I hope we're smart enough to recognize the most wonderful deal ever: By sacrificing our desires, we get to have everything that God wants for us.

> *Those who have sacrificed their homes, relatives, or possessions for my sake will receive a hundred times more and will have eternal life.*
> *— Matthew 19:29*

Ten Thoughts to Ponder
1. Knowing Jesus' name and knowing the person is the difference between merely having a boarding pass and taking flight.
2. We learn the most when we keep trying and failing—never giving up until we eventually succeed.
3. No matter how much I've learned from the past, I need God's foresight to know the next right steps to fulfill his purpose.
4. God's delays aren't denials. His no is never without reason.
5. A wonderful opportunity without perceived value presents itself as a liability not to be pursued.
6. In our walk with the Lord, bad news is a short-sighted misrepresentation of the big picture.
7. When we *hear* God's voice and truly believe, then we have the *doing* that is righteousness according to his nature.
8. The right diet in feasting upon God's Word will make us healthy, wealthy, and wise.
9. We make ourselves a bit smarter, like Einstein, if we can see that until something moves, nothing changes.
10. Sin is what we have when we think wrong is okay and right is merely a matter of interpretation.

Questions for Further Thought
- Why makes it difficult to believe God's plan is better than ours?
- How can we recognize the value of God's rewards?

Stress-Reliever

People work under stress all day, leave for home to face a different kind of stress, then go on a dream vacation to stress on how they are going to pay for all that fun.

We need a stress-reliever where peace isn't postponed and rest isn't earned but can be practiced throughout the day.

You don't have to worry about anything. In prayer and praise, express your desire to God, surrendering to his will, and his peace, which the world cannot understand, will bring calm reassurance through Christ Jesus that everything will be all right.
— Philippians 4:6–7

Ten Thoughts to Ponder

1. Without recognition of a need, we will spend no effort in its pursuit, even though it might be a matter of life and death.
2. No amount of evidence will convince the closed mind that wants to believe otherwise.
3. When we think we already know the truth, the whole truth, and nothing but the truth, our minds are closed to further consideration of the truth.
4. Praise in form is not as good as praise in faith.
5. People who want to hear will hear profoundly better than those who don't want to hear, even though both may have perfect hearing.
6. Some people love their comfort so much that they don't want to know the truth.
7. The moment we lose sight of the value in pursuing whatever God wants, we will pursue what we want.
8. When the Son rises, the Light overcomes the Darkness.
9. Being told I was "going to make it" meant little until I understood that God has something worthwhile for me to make.
10. In a face-to-face meeting with the Lord, people will either be frozen in fear or melted by love.

Questions for Further Thought

- What types of stress are hardest to recognize?
- What habits or thought patterns add stress to our lives?

The Happiness Process

God would be an uncaring Father if he always gave me what I wanted. If I'm expecting riches to make me happy, I have the wrong idea. Jesus said it's next to impossible for a rich person to enter the Kingdom of Heaven. He also said life isn't in the abundance of possessions. I can be happy with less today, if that's what God wants.

More will come on another day.

I have no reason to speak of my needs, because I have learned to be content, no matter what the circumstances are.
— Philippians 4:11

Ten Thoughts to Ponder

1. Extravagant thinking and the possibility of an important discovery requires exploration outside our comfort zone.
2. Being willing to die for the Lord is good, but living for him is better.
3. There is value in ruling out possibilities that don't work so the truth of an impossibility can be discovered, which does work.
4. The greatest futility is desperately searching in all the wrong places.
5. We do well to listen when God says nothing, just for the hope that we will hear when he chooses to speak.
6. When I am unaware of what I don't know, I know a little more when I become aware that I don't know.
7. Knowing and accepting the truth is wonderful. Knowing what to do with the truth is even better.
8. Good intentions are wonderful. Good practice is even better.
9. We don't necessarily need to know how to praise the Lord, but we do necessarily need to do it as best we know how.
10. Believing a lie doesn't make it true, but it does guide our actions as if it were.

Questions for Further Thought

- In what ways do you think happiness is a choice versus a result of circumstances?
- When people are unhappy, what steps would you recommend for finding happiness?

Carefully Crafted

God doesn't use cookie cutters. He handcrafts each of us with care. When we say yes to him with our whole heart, we're in the best place to be shaped to fulfill his perfect plan for our lives.

Surrender to his will turns our ordinary lives into masterpieces, reshaped by grace and made for eternal impact.

I praise you, Lord, because of the awesome, unique way that you created me. You did wonderfully well, and my whole being knows and declares this truth.
— *Psalm 139:14*

Ten Thoughts to Ponder

1. Doing well today can compensate for past errors and prepares for impossible things to be done in the future.
2. When we are hurting, praising the Lord is good, and pleasing him is even better.
3. The strength of God's presence is everywhere, always available—but without open hearts and open minds, we make him completely inaccessible.
4. Foolishness is thinking we can accomplish anything of value without God's help.
5. For success beyond trying, I must have God's help as I realize how I am inept and in desperate need.
6. We don't possess ideas as much as our ideas possess us.
7. Talking about "doing something" does nothing more than "describe something" that isn't happening—not until the *doing* replaces the *talking*.
8. I thought I had a wonderful thought, but then I thought I might think of something better.
9. Sometimes, God allows us to go our own way so we can learn that our own way isn't the best way and choose to follow him.
10. We experience God's love by giving, not getting.

Questions for Further Thought

- How can people discover the unique purpose God has designed for their lives?
- What encouragement can we give to people without hope?

Told to Love

I can't choose to be loved. My being loved was God's choice, not mine, given to me when I wasn't worth loving. He loved me anyway. To really *experience* that love, I must give the love he gave to me.

I must adopt his nature to give like he does, which makes the second commandment as important as the first.

> *You must love God with your whole heart, with all your being and all your strength. ... Love your neighbor as yourself. Of all the commandments, none are greater than these.*
> — Mark 12:30–31

Ten Thoughts to Ponder

1. If you want the most rewarding job and the most understanding and perceptive boss, you should work for the Lord.
2. The Holy Spirit should be our friend, not merely a force to be reckoned with.
3. If we want God's insight to distinguish between the urgent and the important, we should pray a lot.
4. We are thrilled at *receiving* a wonderful gift. Excitement comes in *anticipation* of such a gift.
5. Seminars teach how to organize work, but such a curriculum isn't always suitable for the kind of work we need to do.
6. Religious jargon doesn't do much for our relationship with the Lord, but heartfelt prayer does.
7. For the catching, we need to fish where the fish are, and for the finding, we need to look in all the right places.
8. Without hearing and listening with the desire to learn the truth, there can be no knowing.
9. With the Lord's strength, we don't have to understand *how*, but we must be willing to *do* whatever he guides us to do.
10. The way of the Lord is so profoundly simple that it is hard to grasp, seeming terribly complex.

Questions for Further Thought

- What might make it difficult to experience God's love?
- What challenges arise when trying to love others the way God loves us?

Follow the Leader

According to legend, a colorfully dressed musician used his hypnotic tune to lead all the rats in Hamlin, Germany, to their death in the river. When the king refused to pay for his services as agreed, the pied piper led all the children away, never to be seen again.

We must be careful what we listen to and who we follow.

> *"I am the way, the truth, and the life," Jesus said. "Everyone who reaches the Father goes through me. Enter through the small gate. For many take the wide gate and broad road that lead to destruction. Only a few find the small gate and narrow road that lead to life."*
> — *John 14:6; Matthew 7:13–14*

Ten Thoughts to Ponder

1. I understand that some things are beyond my understanding, but I am still bothered when I don't understand.
2. We have the power to either *radiate* or *restrict* the light of God within us.
3. When we allow ourselves to be used for no good purpose, then our time, money, and effort has been wasted.
4. If we want to … we can praise God for the answer, no matter what it turns out to be.
5. Complete surrender to the Lord's will is the only way to be sure everything is going to be all right.
6. Without God's presence shining through us, we can't be the light of the world.
7. If we're feeling worthless, we should remember the price Jesus paid, just for the chance to have us with him forever.
8. People have good reason to fear for their lives—if they don't know the Lord.
9. We can lose all our joy by counting what we don't have instead of appreciating what we do have.
10. The most wonderful instrument for praising the Lord is our voice.

Questions for Further Thought

- What are the symptoms of a "blind" follower?
- What traits make a leader trustworthy?

Whopper Story

The sudden pull on his fishing line almost jerked the pole out of his hand. "Wow! This one's a whopper. Wait'll I show Dad." Then he remembered … he was supposed to be mowing the yard. "I'm sorry," he said to God. "If I tell my story, I'll have to admit my sin."

After receiving forgiveness for our sins, our stories of what went wrong will show the value of obedience and striving to do what's right.

> *He comforts us during hard times so we may comfort others in similar situations, sharing the hope we had in Christ that brought us through.*
> *— 2 Corinthians 1:4*

Ten Thoughts to Ponder

1. I need to visualize God's sovereignty well enough to know he will cause things to work for good when they don't look good.
2. Reality can be difficult to accept when it is something other than what we want it to be.
3. Asking people for their viewpoint doesn't always reveal what they see. They might say what they think we want to hear.
4. Sticks and stones may break my bones, but God's Word most certainly can heal me.
5. If we understand how much better we can do with God's help, we will be desperate for his strength and guidance.
6. Planning is important only when the work is being done.
7. The reading of God's Word won't help us unless he helps us understand the meaning and how it applies to our lives.
8. Out of our weaknesses come the strength to surrender to God's will.
9. When people ask why they don't see miracles today, the issue is a lack of seeing, not a lack of miracles.
10. Faith allows us to see the God we would otherwise be unable to see.

Questions for Further Thought

- What are the main reasons people feel nervous or hesitant about sharing their testimony with others?
- How can we learn to trust that our stories—no matter how "ordinary"—have the power to inspire or encourage others?

Integrity

I can't get away with anything, no matter how insignificant others might think it is. Why? Because God sees everything I do. I can't bear the thought of displeasing him, but there is another reason. Besides God knowing, I know, and I don't want to live with a liar or a thief.

What others think doesn't matter. God sees me, and I see me, and that's an overwhelming reason to live with integrity.

> *A desire to always please the Lord will take you in the right direction. Doing something else to please yourself will lead to destruction.*
> *— Proverbs 11:3*

Ten Thoughts to Ponder

1. By losing my personal attachments to everything, I have everything to gain personally from the Lord.
2. I thought I knew what I was thinking until I had another thought.
3. Saying "God is love" is an oversimplification, but if I could simplify even more, I might understand what it means.
4. Religion gives people a feeling of salvation without the reality.
5. Without the right value of all the right things, we will find ourselves doing the wrong things for the wrong reasons.
6. Opposite from where God works all things for good, there is another side that isn't so good.
7. Distractions are a problem because we don't see them coming until they've already become a distraction.
8. God allows me to be stupid so I can share God's intelligence that I can take no credit for.
9. With blindness, we fall into the ditch because we don't see the ditch, which explains why we so desperately need the Lord to help our sight.
10. Thinking I can do something without God's help is foolish if not dangerous—or perhaps even fatal.

Questions for Further Thought

- What might make it especially difficult to live with integrity?
- Why do you think people sometimes compromise their values, even when they know it's wrong?

Sovereignty of God

Whether God *causes* or *allows* our distress isn't that important. What really matters is whether we will allow his light to shine through us.

If we can do nothing about our distress, we're left to trust him until the day when he takes it away—and he will. We just don't know when. In the meantime, we should know he isn't guilty of a crime. Why? Because he has a good purpose in all that he causes or allows.

> *We can be thankful for delays that bring patience, because endurance is essential for receiving God's promise.*
> *— Hebrews 10:36*

Ten Thoughts to Ponder

1. God's gifts exceed our ability to comprehend their value—until they are used to help others and we experience some of his great glory.
2. Our actions will expose the lies that we tell to ourselves.
3. If we know we will experience more of God throughout eternity, then we can be excited about whatever lies ahead and thrilled with what we have already received.
4. Without God's direction, dreams are diversions.
5. Talking about desire is easy. Doing what we desire is easy. Changing our desire to all that is good requires God's help.
6. How we feel about our journey depends on what reward we anticipate.
7. Self-sacrifice is not something we will do unless we somehow believe the reward exceeds the cost.
8. The probability of finding is profoundly better when we're looking.
9. We always need God's help, because "Lord, let your will be done, not mine" are easier words to *say* than to do.
10. We know God is older than dirt—because he made the dirt.

Questions for Further Thought

- In what ways might misunderstanding God lead to passivity, fatalism, or a lack of personal responsibility?
- How does faith affect the way we approach disappointment?

Qualified Counselors

Studies have shown the best counseling comes from Christian friends who care. They don't follow counseling rules. They don't even know them. All they know is Jesus, which makes all the difference.

It's not a license on the wall that makes a counselor. It's love from the heart and a deep trust in Jesus, which brings healing that only God can give.

Don't be shy in sharing your stories how Christ has changed your lives, for your reward will be greater than anything you can imagine.
— Hebrews 10:35

Ten Thoughts to Ponder

1. If God is guiding us, we may not be where we think we need to be, but we will be where God knows we need to be.
2. A great story is truth with sound, lights, and action.
3. The best reason to pray is to get what God wants, and the worst is to seek what we want, instead.
4. If God loved us less, he could give us what we want instead of what he knows is best.
5. Tough times that we never wanted can be essential to our becoming more than we could ever dream was possible.
6. Peace is short-lived for those who walk apart from the Lord.
7. We need to hear God's voice, because he knows what we don't know but need to know—and we don't even know what we need to know.
8. As God changes us from glory to glory, we have a taste of even greater miracles ahead.
9. For the work we do, compensation from the Lord wouldn't be worth that much if it only had the form of money.
10. With unbelief, the possible becomes impossible.

Questions for Further Thought

- How can we recognize when someone needs more help than we can provide, and what should we do in those situations?
- How does faith influence the approach and effectiveness of counseling?

Sin City

Sin is available everywhere—in your city, on the Internet, even at church. We can find it anywhere and everywhere. Without immunization, the sin virus will find us, wherever we are.

Why would we ever want to sin? There is no excuse other than to say, "I insist on doing what I want instead of what God wants."

If you listen to God's Spirit within, you will seek to please him and to benefit others, not to satisfy your selfish desires.
— *Galatians 5:16*

Ten Thoughts to Ponder

1. I need God's guidance so I can prepare for the unforeseeable and not waste time getting ready for what won't happen.
2. We should strive to know what is right while knowing we are not always right.
3. When we want to please the Lord, we shouldn't complain when our choices don't turn out how we thought they would.
4. When we are God's captive, we enjoy undefinable freedom.
5. Since God is our Creator, all knowing and all powerful, anything he hasn't caused must be something he has allowed for his good purpose.
6. We won't remain interested in searching if we don't discover the thrill of finding.
7. The right path keeps me going in the same direction until I discover I was wrong and need redirection.
8. God allows us to go our own way so we can discover that it isn't the right way.
9. If our heart is right, desiring the truth at the cost of sacrificing our misbeliefs, we can find God anywhere we look—because he is everywhere.
10. I thought I was doing very well—until I found out that I didn't know what I didn't know and then found more of Jesus, my source of wellness.

Questions for Further Thought

- How is sin most accurately defined?
- In what ways does unconfessed sin affect people?

Crucial Choice

Adam was told not to eat of the Tree of Knowledge of Good and Evil. Eve was told not to touch it. But then Satan came along to make the fruit inviting.

All that looks good isn't always good, which is why we should always depend on the Lord for guidance.

> *I call heaven and earth to witness your choice today, whether for life or death, to be blessed or cursed. Choose life so you and your descendants may live.*
> — *Deuteronomy 30:19*

Ten Thoughts to Ponder

1. Since frustration and joy cannot coexist, we should let go of responsibilities beyond our control and be thankful for God's provision.
2. The self-directed leading the self-directed are like the blind who fall into the ditch.
3. We should know that the greatest threat is the one we can't see, but we often don't see well enough to know that.
4. With God, we can be thankful when everything is not all right—because it will be all right.
5. If I am seeking hidden truth, I need God's help with discovery, because he can see what I cannot see.
6. For God to guide our *thoughts*, not just our *steps*, we need a greater degree of surrender.
7. We may pray for what we want, but we should be most thankful to receive what the Lord wants, instead.
8. Going in circles is exercise going nowhere.
9. We need God's help to know what is possible so we don't waste time looking for something that isn't there.
10. Walking backward is awkward, often dangerous, especially without a rearview mirror.

Questions for Further Thought

- What are the most consequential influences that affect people's choices?
- What can we learn from other people's choices?

Colored Privilege

When little, I rode the bus with my parents. I wanted to stand on the seat at the back, where I could look out the window. Not allowed. Why? I was white. I learned that black people were special, not only getting the best seats on the bus, but they also had their own water fountains and restrooms.

We can be thankful for any colors that might be in our blood, because Jesus loves them all—red, yellow, black, and white.

> *I saw an innumerable multitude from all countries, races, cultures, and languages, standing before the throne and the Lamb, wearing white robes, holding palm branches.*
> — *Revelation 7:9*

Ten Thoughts to Ponder

1. God allows burdens we can't handle so we'll depend on him, who carries loads that we cannot possibly carry on our own.
2. Reward for the pain comes in the harvest of grain.
3. If we're not asleep, we should be awake enough to hear God's voice and follow his direction—or we won't be ready for what lies ahead.
4. One must trust the *process*, or the *prize* will remain a dream.
5. If I'm not looking for what God wants me to see, I will overlook opportunities that would otherwise be obvious.
6. As the point of a pen is pressed upon the paper, so is God's Word impressed upon our hearts.
7. Our time on Earth is too short to be wasted on anything other than what the Lord would have us do.
8. I was thinking about thinking and didn't know what to think—so I dismissed the thought.
9. Scripture is a great resource for truth, but we need God's help with words to reach people who don't believe the Bible.
10. Driving in reverse is disaster without a rearview mirror.

Questions for Further Thought

- How can prejudices exist in our lives without our knowledge?
- How can personal relationships across social, racial, or cultural lines help break down prejudice?

Explosive Moment

I had less than a second to pitch the firecracker before it would explode in my hand. Boom! Suddenly, I was blind and couldn't hear. When my sight returned, I stared into the empty cup. All my firecrackers had exploded at once.

Sometimes our best stories are found in our mistakes that could save others from tragedy.

> *What we have seen and heard is too important to keep quiet.*
> *— Acts 4:20*

Ten Thoughts to Ponder

1. Our ability to embrace misbelief enables us to ignore reality and embrace a fantasy, instead—if that's what we want.
2. Obedience doesn't require understanding, but it does require faith.
3. Talent is overrated, because its development is determined by what we choose to do with our time.
4. Nothing about the future can surprise God and leave him unprepared.
5. Approaching a truth from different perspectives is essential if we want a three-dimensional picture that has depth.
6. We have God's Law to counter Murphy's Law, so all things can work together for good.
7. Since I enjoy being around happy, positive people, I should make a conscious choice to be happy and positive.
8. We need the Lord to help our ignorance, or we will forever remain ignorant and not know it.
9. God has the only agency with a life insurance policy that guarantees a person will not die, and the premiums require total surrender to his will.
10. Pursuit of pleasure can be a fantasy ride lacking worthwhile purpose.

Questions for Further Thought

- Why do personal struggles make stories more meaningful and memorable?
- What kinds of stories are the most life-changing?

Path to Being Great

"God helps those who help themselves." Some Christians think that old saying is biblical. We might do better if we show how helping others is the best way to help ourselves. God made us to do that, and we're worthless to him if we don't.

Scripture says God helps those who help others, not those who help themselves.

> *Whoever is the greatest among you must be everyone's servant. Those who try to make themselves great will be humbled, and those who humble themselves will be exalted.*
> — Matthew 23:11–12

Ten Thoughts to Ponder
1. People want control when they think God won't give them what they want, when they want it, and how they want it.
2. Complaining about the past is a waste of hot air.
3. The answer with all things considered can be significantly different from when only a few things are considered.
4. A bad goal is worse than no goal at all, and without God's help, we won't know the difference.
5. When I only *think* I understand, my misunderstanding makes me think something is simple when it is actually complex.
6. The best way to make a lie convincing is to make it assumed without question.
7. The difficulty with understanding is not understanding how much we don't know and don't know we don't know.
8. The Holy Spirit leads us to see what we otherwise would not see—but only if we want to see it.
9. Where we think the fish are is not necessarily where they really are—unless we can see below the surface.
10. What captures your attention ... captures your heart.

Questions for Further Thought
- Why is *greatness* different in the Kingdom of God?
- How does our natural desire for recognition or praise get in the way of genuine service?

Slap in the Face

As a kid, I was shoved to the ground a few times, but I never rose up to fight. When my sandwich was stolen, I acted like I was glad someone else had it. When kicked, I didn't react.

Daddy was right. Not only did the bullies soon leave me alone. They respected me for my strength.

> *Don't retaliate, insulting or injuring others after they have done that to you, but do the opposite, blessing them, for you will be blessed when you bless others.*
> *— 1 Peter 3:9*

Ten Thoughts to Ponder

1. Eventually, lies are self-defeating, because a multitude of lies made to look like the truth will never become truth.
2. After 2,000 years, Jesus is still worthy of celebration.
3. With the hope of deceiving those who can be deceived, Satan appears as an angel of light when he is actually filled with the darkest evil.
4. The best shoulder to cry on is the Lord's.
5. I need God's help because the things I need to forget are so easily remembered, and the things I need to remember are so easily forgotten.
6. When we don't have much to offer, we should remember that God can do a lot with a little.
7. Forgetfulness is an issue when we don't remember what we have forgotten or why it needs to be remembered.
8. God makes impossibilities into probabilities.
9. We cannot improve on the invitation God has to offer, but we certainly can improve the way we deliver those invitations.
10. If you're eager to hear good news, abandon cable news and read the Bible more.

Questions for Further Thought

- Why is it so hard to resist the urge to retaliate when someone hurts or insults us?
- How does trusting God's justice help us let go of the need to "get even"?

Harvesters

Edward Kimball led Dwight Moody to the Lord, but Edward was not able to lead his own son Henry to the Lord. That happened under the ministry of Dwight Moody, during one of his evangelistic campaigns.

Taking credit for "leading people to the Lord" is like the harvesters who did little work compared to the cultivators, weeders, waterers, and pruners who preceded the harvest.

The one who plants works with the one who waters, each one seeing the benefit of his work in the harvest.
— 1 Corinthians 3:8

Ten Thoughts to Ponder

1. The truth can be preached, but it can't be proven, because there's always somebody who can choose not to believe.
2. I am limited by who I am—unless God will help me become better than I am.
3. In Christ, we can play the hypocrite, or we can be authentic, but *acting authentic* is impossible, a contradiction of terms.
4. The problem with goals is looking so far ahead that we can't see the next right step.
5. Since God has already made every possible move toward us, it's our responsibility to take the next step toward him.
6. Creativity will relentlessly seek a way—for as long as it believes there is a way.
7. The purpose of *service* is to serve those who need to be served, with the hope that they too might learn the eternal value of serving others.
8. When standing with Jesus, we can hear God say, "Not guilty."
9. People who think they can "fake it until they make it" wind up living in a fantasy world as a fake person.
10. In the midst of darkness, the Bible is our searchlight to discover the truth.

Questions for Further Thought

- How can we avoid comparing our work to someone else's?
- In what ways can we encourage others and celebrate those who seem small but are essential to the harvest?

Stress Reliever

When tempted to *run* from stress, I press on, instead. Invariably, either I learn that I had a hyperactive imagination and no real problem existed, or I discover solutions. Either way, I've done what I can. I don't have to stress.

In conflict, silence is never golden, because stress keeps building until that explosive moment when we say or do something we regret.

> *Don't think you can decide on your own what is best for you. Respect what the Lord says you should do, and refuse to do wrong, which will bring health to your body and strength to your bones.*
> *— Proverbs 3:7–8*

Ten Thoughts to Ponder

1. We need God's help to be only concerned with the things we need to be concerned about.
2. Worry doesn't change anything—but prayer can.
3. In effective communication, a person must cross an emotional bridge beginning from the opposite side, where the audience is.
4. Claiming what we don't have is self-deception that prevents our having what we claim.
5. The one who came to steal, kill, and destroy will do all he can to help those who support his kingdom.
6. Jesus' words will either save or condemn us, depending on how well we listen.
7. No matter the magnitude of a problem, there is always one small step in the right direction that will work toward resolution.
8. There is never a time we don't need to pray, because we need the Lord's help all the time.
9. Under control, energy has the power for us to turn the other cheek, but out of control, we will strike back with vengeance.
10. Without movement, there can be no momentum.

Questions for Further Thought

- What are the biggest sources of stress?
- How can you best help those who are fearful and anxious?

Worthwhile Effort

I must habitually challenge my mind in the right direction, telling myself that the effort is worth the pain. It's a game I must win, because if I don't believe in a great reward for the effort, I'll quit.

Unless we believe in God and the rewards that follow, we'll neither approach him nor will we seek to please him.

> *Never tire of doing good, for a harvest of blessing is certain if you never give up on God.*
> *— Galatians 6:9*

Ten Thoughts to Ponder

1. While agonizing over not having more, I can miss the opportunity to do what God wants, using what I already have.
2. Doing God's will would be easy if it weren't so hard to change our desires not to do it.
3. If Satan wasn't satisfying a purpose God has for him going about as a roaring lion seeking whom he might devour, then God wouldn't allow Satan to be here.
4. We think we know what "trusting God" means until tests reveal how much we don't yet know.
5. Our actions reveal a lot of truth about our motivation—and the lies that we might be telling ourselves.
6. Of all those we need to effectively communicate with, we most need to communicate with God.
7. The path where God takes us will look crooked until we see how he is taking us directly to where he wants us to be.
8. Where there is no will, there is no way.
9. If we are open and honest with ourselves, we have a much better chance for others to believe what we have to say.
10. When God helps us *be* good, we don't have to worry about *looking* good.

Questions for Further Thought

- How does faith shape our ability to endure difficult seasons without giving up?
- What are some practical ways to stay motivated when you can't yet see the results of your efforts?

Fully Committed

I was once told that 10 percent belongs to the Lord, which I now think is great Old Testament thinking. God isn't asking for a percentage. He desires everything we are and all we have, holding nothing back.

When we live 100 percent committed, generosity, obedience, and trust naturally follow, not out of obligation but out of love.

> *I beg you, all who have said they want to follow the Lord, make a total commitment to please him in all things, sacrificing everything you want so you may receive something better. Your reasonable service is giving 100 percent of yourself, more than just a tithe, a few worship songs, and verbal expressions of your love for him.*
> — Romans 12:1

Ten Thoughts to Ponder

1. The most important area of creativity is being creative enough to creatively seek ways to be more creative.
2. Some people are too busy talking to listen effectively.
3. We need faith to understand that our needs are different from what we want.
4. Assumptions are easily overlooked obstacles that oppose effective communication.
5. The goal of enticement is to make the audience believe it has no choice but to buy what has been advertised.
6. When we fully surrender to the Lord, our needs change, so we no longer need a spanking.
7. With just one simple thought, we can expand the concept and write 30,000 words of complexity made simple.
8. The most important thing about importance ... is understanding what's important.
9. Since God provides the means for everyone to know the truth, we have no excuse for choosing not to know the truth.
10. Compared to eternity, our lifespan on Earth is immeasurably close to zero.

Questions for Further Thought

- What are the biggest obstacles to full surrender to God's will?
- How does trusting God help us commit to his will?

Treasure Chest

The rare "Inverted Jenny," a postage stamp with an upside-down biplane, sold at auction for over two million dollars. An 1856 one-cent stamp from British Guiana sold for 9.5 million. I'm amazed at what collectors will bid for something that will be locked away, unused.

Where we invest our time, energy, and resources speaks volumes about what we truly hold dear.

> *The Kingdom of Heaven is like hidden treasure buried in a field. When a man found the treasure, he was overcome with joy. He buried the treasure, sold everything he owned, and bought the field.*
> *— Matthew 13:44*

Ten Thoughts to Ponder

1. With Jesus, we can be full and satisfied, yet hunger for more.
2. If we don't think we have a purpose, then there is nothing worthwhile to pursue, and we become professional wanderers.
3. Effective communicators will pay attention to their ineffective communication and keep looking until they find a solution.
4. Without the Lord, anywhere we go should be frightening.
5. Hypocrisy is like a dirty window where people on the outside can't see in, but looking out from the inside is difficult, as well.
6. A letter to God doesn't require postage.
7. The complexity of the situation leaves me knowing I need to trust the Lord, because he alone understands all things.
8. Believing in the value of a goal will add pleasure and willingness to endure the pain that is unavoidable if we are to achieve the prize.
9. If we are completely surrendered to the Lord's redirection, we can be confident that we will arrive at the right place at the right time.
10. Until we make the choice to trust God, we cannot know how trustworthy God really is.

Questions for Further Thought

- What do you think are people's worst kinds of investments?
- How can we determine our best use of time and money?

Best Friend

Some people don't think they have a *best* friend and worry about being unfriended. I've lost friends who had better things to do with their time. I've been unfriended, neglected, and betrayed. Some have died.

Friends come and go, but we never have to feel alone, because our heavenly Father is the best friend we could ever have.

> *You don't have to fear anything or anyone if your Lord God is with you. You never have to be alone, because he will never abandon you. Just don't ever forsake him.*
> — Deuteronomy 31:6

Ten Thoughts to Ponder

1. Part of enjoying simplicity is the opportunity to explore the complex and can see it simplified, so we can then enjoy the illusion of complete understanding.
2. Those who truly know the Lord are already taking early steps in their journey throughout eternity.
3. As faith without works is dead, so is planning without doing.
4. God doesn't promise strength for every *possible* task, but he always supplies strength for every *appointed* task.
5. In walking with the Lord, we can find great pleasure in having less, but without the Lord, having more is never enough.
6. Pride says I am somebody, when the truth is, without God, I wouldn't be anything of value.
7. I am frustrated because I am so frustrated that I cannot get rid of my frustration.
8. We think we know what we're saying, and others think they know what we are saying, but both of us could be wrong.
9. God is a specialist in helping us with our specialties that he has given especially for us.
10. The miracle of God's promises is seeing no way they can be fulfilled, but God makes a way, anyway.

Questions for Further Thought

- What are the most important qualities to have in a friend?
- How does social media impact the authenticity of friendships?

Sin No More

After forgiveness, Jesus told people to "go and sin no more." I wonder how well they did, whether their struggles continued.

With forgiveness, *past* sins might be forgotten, but *present* sin will persist when we're not fully surrendered to God's will. Without daily surrender, sin finds a way to settle back in.

Trash your old ways that are garbage, corrupted by deceptive desires, and let the Holy Spirit transform your thoughts and actions. Become the new person God wants you to be, righteous and holy.
— Ephesians 4:22–24

Ten Thoughts to Ponder
1. Some people give to the Lord of their financial resources, but the greater sacrifice is the gift of our time.
2. As we gain greater appreciation for God's gifts, we have greater appreciation for who God is.
3. The best way to have confidence in doing better is to enjoy the means by which we are *already* doing better.
4. If we understand Psalms, we should know how to pray.
5. Faith is knowing what cannot possibly be known without first choosing to believe.
6. If you want to be more like God, then seek to care more about people, especially your enemies.
7. The wonderful thing about praising God is getting to experience his presence in the process.
8. Without relentless searching, the probability of discovery approaches zero.
9. We should treasure the process of learning as much as we enjoy the discoveries, because without the process, there could be no learning.
10. When God is for us, our only chance for failure is to ignore his call and choose to give up.

Questions for Further Thought
- After receiving forgiveness, why do people struggle with sin?
- How can we protect ourselves from falling back into old patterns of sin?

Journey of a Lifetime

I sometimes hear Christians talk about being "born again" as if a *profession* of faith ends the journey. Actually, it's only the beginning.

Salvation is more than a past event. It's an ongoing transformation. We are saved, being saved, and will be saved—an unfolding process that calls for faithfulness and growth.

> *Like someone looking into a mirror, we see the beauty of who we will become, more and more like the Lord, being changed from glory to even greater glory by the work of his Spirit.*
> *— 2 Corinthians 3:18*

Ten Thoughts to Ponder

1. The sooner we can learn from the process, the more quickly we can avoid the pain and enjoy the pleasure.
2. Faith is the catalyst that prompts us to do more than we thought we could or should do.
3. We pray without ceasing, not so we can have more gifts, but so we can know how to best use what we have been given.
4. A light can receive no credit for its radiance unless it is allowed to shine.
5. We most need the desire to learn and use what we've learned, because without the desire, what we already know will soon be forgotten.
6. The success of God's plan depends on doing our part so he can do his part.
7. People often think forgiving others is a sign of weakness, but actually, it's a sign of God-given strength.
8. We would not seek comfort in the Lord if it were not for our discomfort.
9. If we can be confident in the Lord's Word, then we can have high expectations for what he might do in us.
10. A great story told is a life made bold.

Questions for Further Thought

- Why might people see salvation as a one-time event instead of a lifelong process?
- What does it mean to "work out your salvation"?

Satisfaction

My early pursuits of pleasure often brought disappointment, not satisfaction. Why? Enough was never enough. When the thrill faded, the emptiness returned. I had to learn to surrender my desires to the Lord.

True satisfaction begins, not with gaining more, but with surrendering to the One who made us for himself.

> *A lover of silver will not be satisfied with silver. If wealth is your goal, you will never have enough. You might as well be chasing the wind.*
> *— Ecclesiastes 5:10*

Ten Thoughts to Ponder

1. If we want to become like Jesus, we should develop his addiction to pleasing the Father above anything or anyone else.
2. God loves our praise because of all the good it will do for us.
3. When we don't embrace the truth as it really is, we are embracing a lie while telling ourselves it is the truth.
4. God will not respect a prayer that asks for something we do not really want.
5. Those who have everything but still aren't satisfied should admit that their wants were not their needs.
6. We should praise God for what he has done, what he is doing, and what he will yet do.
7. To be the victor and not the victim, we need to listen to God's voice and ignore other voices that would lead us astray.
8. If we recognize as God whatever he whispers to our hearts, then we open the door to hearing more from him, and not something we choose to imagine.
9. Many employers don't really know the quality of the work we are doing, but when we're working for the Lord, he knows better than we do.
10. Identifying a problem is good, but there is no reward until we find the solution.

Questions for Further Thought

- Why is it sometimes hard to trust that God is enough?
- How can unmet desires or delayed answers to prayer shape our understanding of where true satisfaction comes from?

Understanding Service

When a father was asked about the plaque in the church lobby, honoring our military, he said. "That's for us to remember the soldiers who died in the service." The son looked both surprised and concerned. "Which one? Morning or evening?"

In a church *service*, we should consider the kinds of sacrifices we really are making.

> *Your reasonable service is giving 100 percent of yourself, more than just a tithe, a few worship songs, and verbal expressions of your love for him.*
> — Romans 12:1

Ten Thoughts to Ponder

1. If we want to know the time, it's a good idea to have a clock, and then ask God for what should come next.
2. Without faith, trusting God is impossible, because we think we need to be in control.
3. The difficulty with distractions is that their unexpected arrival comes too late to say we didn't want to accept it.
4. Time is like money. If we don't keep track of where it's spent, we don't know where it went.
5. We must first recognize our need. Then, we can see the importance of the action that will satisfy that need.
6. If Jesus hadn't fully submitted to God's will, he could not have been without sin.
7. With a desire to improve, we'll not get worse. And if we're not getting worse, we *must* be getting better.
8. As we walk with God, our tragedies will become triumphs.
9. Since God wants to be found, he will always make himself findable as we seek after him.
10. Prayer without ceasing is needed to overcome an unhealthy addiction.

Questions for Further Thought

- What is the difference between genuine sacrifice and routine religious activity?
- How do we know if our sacrifices please God?

Encouragement

Life has no shortage of trials and disappointments. When hardships come, we look for meaning—and when we don't find it, despair can sneak in. But God sees the end from the beginning. His promises are sure, and his plans are perfect—even when they're hidden.

Encouragement flows from truth, and truth reminds us that God isn't finished. His purposes are greater than our problems.

With God fighting for us, we cannot lose as long as we maintain our desire to please him.
— Romans 8:31

Ten Thoughts to Ponder
1. Of all teachers, the Lord is by far the best at targeting life's lessons to be perfectly suited for each individual's need.
2. In working for the Lord, we will never have an employer who cares for us more than he does.
3. When we become discouraged, the Lord will provide ample opportunities for us to be encouraged—if we want to be.
4. Effective communicators learn to carry on a meaningful conversation with themselves.
5. When we work for the Lord, our work goes with us wherever we go, because he is always with us to help us do the work.
6. If we surrender our desires, working for the Lord can be like vacation every day of the year.
7. Praying for God to give us what we want is missing the valuable process of searching and discovering what God wants.
8. Believing in God's will above our own will place confidence where it belongs.
9. Working for God is good because we don't have to *worry* about anything.
10. If we don't have faith in God's plan, we're looking for someone or something to blame.

Questions for Further Thought
- How does encouragement differ from simple compliments or flattery?
- Why is encouragement more productive than criticism?

Never Alone

In a stadium filled with people, without a single empty seat anywhere around us, where everyone is a stranger, we can still feel alone. The presence of a person isn't enough. We need the relationships.

God is close enough to know our thoughts at all times. But without a relationship, we might not be aware that he's anywhere around.

Where could I go and not find your Spirit there? Is there anywhere I could escape your presence?
— *Psalm 139:7*

Ten Thoughts to Ponder
1. Since time travel is an impossibility, we waste our time wishing the past had been different or worrying about the future that we can't control.
2. The poor might think they need riches, but the rich know that isn't enough.
3. What I want needs to be what God knows I need, which is different from what I want and think I need.
4. We can anticipate a mansion in Heaven, but without Jesus, we won't see the city, let alone our street.
5. Pray without ceasing, because God already knows what we want and what we need—and with prayer, we can know what we need and should want.
6. People who idolize money as a blessing are likely to lose it.
7. At the heart of salvation is choosing to love God's voice and also follow his direction above all other voices.
8. Having great love of those who would choose to follow him instead of their own way was something God saw as worth dying for.
9. When we think we need what we want, we will miss seeing what we should want but don't know we need.
10. Since we cannot deceive God, the best hope for our hypocrisy is to deceive ourselves.

Questions for Further Thought
- How does loneliness differ from simply being alone?
- What are the main causes of loneliness today?

Right Fear

Since Satan can roar and roam only where God allows, we should be most concerned about God's purpose. Believers shouldn't give the enemy more attention than he deserves, fearing his schemes as if he has free rein. Satan is on a leash, permitted only to do what God allows.

Our security isn't in knowing the devil's limits. It's in trusting God's sovereignty. When we fix our eyes on his purpose, fear of the enemy fades, and faith rises in its place.

> *Lord, you are my light of knowledge, wisdom, and inspiration. You are my salvation from all that would pull me down, so who is left for me to fear? My life is in your hands, so I have no reason to be afraid.*
> — Psalm 27:1

Ten Thoughts to Ponder

1. Without God's help, we will never get from where we are to where he wants us to be.
2. Our hope for finding our way depends upon God showing us.
3. If we want to experience the goodness of God, we must go his way, not ours.
4. A weak God connection lacks sufficient power for a person's light to shine brightly.
5. God uses the weak and the worthless to work his miracles.
6. The more we empty ourselves of ourselves, the more capacity we have for radiating God's glorious light.
7. Only a Good Shepherd can appreciate the value of a lost lamb.
8. Those who discover the great value of helping others should always be looking for ways to *help others help others.*
9. The cross would be meaningless if it weren't for the empty tomb.
10. We might as well admit that God is in control, and we're not—because God is in control, and we're not.

Questions for Further Thought

- How can focus on God's purpose reduce fear of the enemy?
- What practical steps can help you shift your focus from fear of the enemy to faith in God?

No Other Way

Heaven has no backdoor entrance. In a world that celebrates many paths and personal truths, Jesus' claim is unapologetically exclusive. He is the way, truth, and life.

Jesus is the only door giving access to the Father. No amount of good works, spiritual effort, or religious sincerity can bypass the cross.

> *Because of Jesus Christ, people everywhere have access by the Holy Spirit to our Father God.*
> *— Ephesians 2:18*

Ten Thoughts to Ponder

1. Many things look good to us because somebody found the right bait for the hook.
2. We might as well be open and honest with God, because he knows us better than we know ourselves.
3. We have an unusual form of willpower when we choose to surrender to God's will when nothing is forcing us to make that choice.
4. If we're waiting for the perfect moment to start, the job will never be done.
5. We must trust the Lord and sacrifice what we want, or we will never learn how valuable and pleasure-filled his ways can be.
6. When we are unsure of our next step, we should at least be preparing to take another step.
7. With the Lord guiding our steps, we should not be surprised to see closed doors open for no apparent reason.
8. Finding a piece in a picture puzzle is a convenient thrill of discovery—much easier than working through our struggles to find what's missing in our lives.
9. If we want to enjoy life, we should find pleasure in doing all the things we must do.
10. Manufacturers have molds and dies to make everything alike, but our Creator has the genius to make everything unique.

Questions for Further Thought

- Why do people resist the idea that Jesus is the only way?
- What heart issues might lie behind that resistance?

The Gift That Uses Us

The gift of God's presence is unusual because, instead of using his gift for our glory, the gift uses us for his glory. Some gifts are ours to enjoy as we see fit. But the gift of God's presence is different.

The Holy Spirit is not a tool we wield. His presence leads, guides, and empowers us for his work.

> *If you who are evil know how to give good gifts to your children, you can be sure your heavenly Father will give the Holy Spirit to those who ask him.*
> — Luke 11:13

Ten Thoughts to Ponder

1. Unconditional love has capacity for judgment but has no place for hatred.
2. If we don't know how to get somewhere, we become dependent upon whoever or whatever can show us the way.
3. We assume that we know how to pray, because we think we know what we want.
4. If God were to fill out a tax return, I would be delighted if he would show me as one of his dependents and how much he paid for my support.
5. The great problem with my ignorance is not knowing what question to ask so I can know.
6. We need to recognize God as more than the *giver* of life, because his being our *sustainer* of life is most important.
7. God has no need to give us more than we need, but Satan might, so we would go our own way.
8. I am more intelligent when I know how little I know, but for lack of comparison, it's not easy to know how little I know.
9. Like with Abraham and Sarah, trusting God's Word will overcome our unbelief.
10. As we walk in faith, unexpected doors lead to holy ground.

Questions for Further Thought

- How can we discern between our desires and the leading of the Holy Spirit?
- What role does humility play in God using us for his purpose?

Light in the Darkness

I can't share one of my books if I don't carry one with me. That seems obvious, but the same truth applies to our words of encouragement. We can't offer hope without first having hope in our hearts.

As the light of the world, we must be filled with God's presence, so his light naturally shines through us to those who need it most.

> *Make good on your commitment to the Lord by preparing to share your experiences with those who might not understand how you have survived your struggles. Always be ready to reveal why you have hope in this tumultuous world.*
> *— 1 Peter 3:15*

Ten Thoughts to Ponder

1. To receive the promise, we need patience, because our sense of timing isn't as good as God's.
2. By always doing what's right, you can never go wrong.
3. Perfect timing requires prayer without ceasing, with the desire for God to be our constant guide.
4. Both Christians and unbelievers pursue pleasures—but in opposite directions, either toward or away from God.
5. The thrill of being used of God is knowing we're not that good—but he is.
6. To wait upon the Lord means to expect him to do a new thing and discover how we should act accordingly.
7. Walking with the Lord means we can be excited, even when facing the fiery furnace.
8. With the Lord's help, we can put our losses behind us—so we no longer have to take them with us.
9. The more we praise God, the more we can see his miracles and have justification for our praise.
10. We should be excited about today, because we can do something that will make tomorrow better.

Questions for Further Thought

- What are some practical ways we can keep encouragement ready to give, just as we might carry a book to share?
- How do people distinguish true from fake encouragement?

Weight of His Cross

Jesus couldn't carry his own cross, not because he lacked spiritual power, but because he bore the full weight of human frailty.

His collapse becomes our call: to take up his cross daily—not just to suffer but to surrender fully. True life in Christ doesn't comes through sacrifice, and resurrection power follows a crucified will.

> *Those who will not take up their cross and follow in my footsteps cannot be my disciples.*
> *— Luke 14:27*

Ten Thoughts to Ponder

1. Scripture should be encouraging—if we're on God's side.
2. Trash is anything that's of no use, destined for the dumpster—so we'd do well to make ourselves useful to the Lord.
3. Without patient anticipation for what God wants next, we will miss the promise, because we will take our own action instead of following his direction.
4. Nothing could be more confusing than hearing the wrong thing and thinking it's right or hearing the right thing and thinking it's wrong.
5. If we find ways to enjoy our work, we'll do a better job.
6. When our desire to know the truth is real and relentless, God will give us the means to distinguish the truth from a lie.
7. To break a bad addiction and create a good one, address the forces that drive your desires.
8. For as long as we agonize over wanting what we don't have, we deprive ourselves of God's pleasure providing our needs.
9. Pleasing the Lord with what we have allows him to accomplish more than we thought possible.
10. Time is like having a dollar per minute, and every hour is a $60 loss if we don't use it for something worthwhile.

Questions for Further Thought

- How might recognizing Jesus' physical weakness on the way to the cross shape the way we view our own weaknesses?
- What does it mean to "take up our cross daily"?

The Long Road with God

God never intended to be our once-a-week companion. More than the sanctuary, his presence is for the sidewalks, hills, and highways of life.

If we really do want him, not just for a moment but forever, he will never leave our side. He delights in consistent communion and desires a relationship marked by daily reliance upon him.

> *I will always be with you, even until the end of the world.*
> — *Matthew 28:20*

Ten Thoughts to Ponder

1. We do better when we are inspired to work, because that makes the effort more fun.
2. If I can know how little I know, then I can know how much I need to be dependent upon what God knows.
3. In *looking* for inspiration, we do well to *stir up* the inspiration we already have.
4. We might think we need to avoid temptation, but actually, we need spiritual strength to walk through it, unharmed.
5. Since God knows the end from the beginning, he alone is qualified to tell us where we are.
6. Recognizing God's presence, we are compelled to do what that presence is calling us to do. Or not to do.
7. Excitement is a wonderful thrill when it reflects our progress in moving within God's will.
8. God will play Hide and Seek with the hope that we will hunger for his presence and look for him.
9. Waiting upon the Lord has the important element of doing whatever it takes to find out what we should be doing.
10. A *desire* to hear and follow the Lord is as important as hearing and following the Lord, because we cannot have one without the other.

Questions for Further Thought

- How might we encourage others to see God not as a "Sunday companion" but as a daily friend and guide?
- How does knowing God is at your side affect your confidence in facing challenges?

Change of Heart

In fulfilling the Law, Jesus raised our behavior standards above what laws require. While the Law focused on external obedience, Jesus pointed to internal transformation. Anger becomes murder. Lust becomes adultery.

His expectations are humanly impossible—unless we receive a heart transplant through the Spirit.

> *Unless your righteousness is greater than the righteousness of the Pharisees and teachers of the Law, there is no way you will enter the Kingdom.*
> — Matthew 5:20

Ten Thoughts to Ponder
1. The more we live in God's truth, the more we can recognize the lie that appears to be true.
2. What we need is God, in whatever form he makes himself available, but to find out what that is, we must make *ourselves* available.
3. In Heaven, Jesus is the head of Human Resources.
4. We should not be surprised if turntables turn, snakes bite, or God loves—because it is their nature.
5. With unconditional surrender, we declare ourselves totally dependent upon the Lord.
6. Form without faith is a fatal deception.
7. When looking for inspiration, start with people's needs that you might be able to satisfy.
8. If we knew how much God's ways are above ours, we might accept the reality that our truth can fall short of his truth.
9. Knowing where to look is the most important part of finding.
10. If we ever think God doesn't hear our prayers, we should know that God knows our thoughts as well as our prayers.

Questions for Further Thought
- How does equating anger with murder, or lust with adultery, change the way we view sin?
- What does it mean to receive a "heart transplant" through the Spirit?

Imaginary Friend

I was never alone. As a child, I often talked to my imaginary friend. He was always eager to hear what I had to say, always understanding how I felt.

God isn't a childish fantasy. He is more real than anyone we can see with our eyes. We do well to talk to him. All the time.

> *Those who know and respect the Lord will treasure their relationship with him, a mystery that others cannot figure out.*
> *— Psalm 25:14*

Ten Thoughts to Ponder

1. The worst weakness is feeling we can't do what the Lord would have us do, because he'll supply the strength we need.
2. What we do matters little, compared to the love that should be expressed in doing it.
3. The best way to prepare for a future we cannot possibly foresee is to follow God's guidance for today.
4. The crucial element for knowing truth is the *desire* to know. Without that desire, we will embrace an artificial reality.
5. All we've heard about Jesus isn't enough until we actually know him.
6. If we fail to wait upon the Lord, we will have the perfect example of our independent effort in doing what we should not have done.
7. The sheep who know their shepherd's voice are never lost.
8. If we're not seeing the love, wisdom, and power of God, we should pray for our eyes to be opened.
9. If we think we're beyond repair, we should remember that God can fix stuff that we can't fix.
10. God knew "the love of those who would choose to follow him instead of their own way" was worth dying for.

Questions for Further Thought

- Why might God prefer to call us friends instead of followers or servants?
- What are the qualifications for a person to be called a "friend of God?"

Cause for Surrender

We can't surrender what we cannot see.

Often, our pride and blind spots keep areas of rebellion hidden. But as we walk with Jesus, his light reveals deeper levels of needed surrender—not to shame us, but to free us. His illumination invites transformation.

> *Search me thoroughly, God. Examine my heart, and check to be sure my thoughts are pure. If you see in me anything offensive, put me on the right path to pleasing you.*
> — Psalm 139:23–24

Ten Thoughts to Ponder

1. Desperate for present pleasures, people will ignore the consequence of their behavior that will ultimately lead to death.
2. The important difference between *tools* and *toys* is the value of their service.
3. If we want to do well with our struggles, we must hear God's voice and then do our best to obey.
4. Even before we know to ask the question, God has the right answer ready.
5. If we seek the Lord in prayer without ceasing, we have a direct connection to know difficult but life-changing truths.
6. Confronted with truth, we face a choice whether we will believe or not believe.
7. Until we let go of the things we need to let go of, we cannot embrace the things that we need to embrace.
8. When we have fully loved God, then we are fully equipped to love people as we should.
9. Trusting God means following his plan when we aren't sure where we're headed or what the plan is.
10. Praising God in our tragedies will open the door to experiencing his triumphs.

Questions for Further Thought

- How do you distinguish between conviction from God and self-condemnation?
- What kinds of fear make surrender difficult?

Victory in Advance

Christians can celebrate before the war is over because victory is guaranteed.

God cannot lose. Faith doesn't wait for physical evidence. It shouts victory while still surrounded by uncertainty. In Christ, our triumph is assured, even if our circumstances haven't caught up yet.

Thankfully, through our Lord Jesus Christ, God has given us victory over wrongdoing and death. Therefore, my good friends, be strong in the Lord, passionate about doing his work, knowing that your effort will always have great value.
— *1 Corinthians 15:57–58*

Ten Thoughts to Ponder

1. Life insurance policies are written for someone other than the policyholder—except for the one we can have with the Lord.
2. As well as prayer without ceasing, we need to be about our Master's business without ceasing.
3. To be lost but not know we are lost can be tragic, because the Lord can't find those who don't want to be found.
4. With the resurrection of Jesus, the grace of God became *amazing* grace.
5. Those who love darkness and are repulsed by the light are identified by the shining of God's light through his people.
6. For the light to have value, there must be darkness.
7. Physical maladies are nothing compared to the spiritual and emotional ailments that would separate us from God.
8. Since God knows the future, he can never make a mistake in judgment.
9. If we want to believe a lie, we will see the truth as a lie and the lie as the truth. We'll be difficult to convince that we're wrong.
10. Without a desire for God's help, we are not going to become who God wants us to be.

Questions for Further Thought

- Why might people insist on physical evidence before trusting God?
- What aspects of Jesus' life give you the most confidence?

Truth That Sets Us Straight

Preaching without practicing truth leads to self-deception.

It's easy to impress others with godly words, yet live with a divided heart. When actions and beliefs don't align, we need a fresh outpouring of truth—not just to teach others, but to correct ourselves.

Don't just hear God's voice as if that's enough, deceiving yourselves. Listen to him, and then do what he wants.
— James 1:22

Ten Thoughts to Ponder
1. Words shouldn't be judged as truth only because of their appearance, for Satan himself appears as an angel of light.
2. If we know but don't know that we know, we still live in ignorance.
3. The most creative story we can write is the pursuit of whatever God wants, because it's filled with mystery and suspense, with a most rewarding conclusion.
4. Failure is the easiest goal, because all we have to do is quit.
5. Omnipotence without omniscience is like a bull in a china closet—destructive and dangerous. Thankfully, God is not only all-powerful but also all-knowing.
6. Believing we will have a bad day can easily become a self-fulfilling prophecy.
7. For access to Heaven, my identity will be my password, and if I don't have the right identity in my relationship with the Lord, I'm not getting in.
8. For as long as we see ourselves as great, we will have difficulty seeing how great God is.
9. Asking for God's direction won't tell us which way to go—unless we really do want to know his way and not our way.
10. For those who choose to go their own way, God's promises are threatening, not thrilling.

Questions for Further Thought
- How can someone preach truth yet fall into self-deception?
- What are the dangers of impressing others with godly language without living it out?

Uprooted

God has the power to uproot and replant our lives—shifting us into new callings, new places, and new seasons that we could never reach on our own. His hand is steady, his wisdom flawless, and his timing perfect. But one thing he will never do is force our surrender.

Willingness is the soil where transformation grows. When we release our grip on the familiar—our routines, our comforts, even our fears—we make room for God to plant something better.

> *"Every plant that was not planted by my heavenly Father will be pulled up with its roots," Jesus said.*
> *— Matthew 15:13*

Ten Thoughts to Ponder

1. We can be thankful that God knows what he is doing, because that knowledge can free us from worry over our not knowing.
2. Claiming to know Jesus isn't enough to save us if all we know is the name.
3. Those who view prayer as a means to complete a transaction have not yet learned the importance of the relationship.
4. The best way to experience God's blessing is to bless others.
5. To alleviate our ignorance, we need to relentlessly research with the hope of finding whatever we need to know.
6. The best preparation for the future is faithfulness today.
7. A box filled with tools is of no use if we don't open the box and get the tool that perfectly suits the need.
8. Walking with the Lord is an endless pleasure-filled adventure—if we choose to enjoy it.
9. If we want to be part of the popular "ignorance club," we must appear to be more ignorant than we really are.
10. Hearing nice things about ourselves is wonderful—and it's even better when they are true.

Questions for Further Thought

- What emotions surface when you think about God "uprooting" and replanting your life in a new direction?
- What fears most often cause people to cling to the familiar instead of trusting God's replanting?

About the Author

Frank Ball was born in Kansas and became a naturalized Texan after moving to the Gulf Coast in 1954. After high school graduation, his forty-dollars-a-week salary as an office supply deliveryman required careful management. Half went to help support his parents, three younger brothers, and two sisters. The rest paid his ten-dollar-per-month car payment, filled the gas tank for less than 20 cents per gallon, and left a little pocket change for fun. Success came the old-fashioned way. He earned it.

Computer programming and business administration paid the bills. But in 1992, he began to abandon that love to pursue excellence in what he had most hated—writing—so he could compile a story for people who had heard of Jesus but didn't know much about what he said and did.

For ten years, he directed North Texas Christian Writers to help members improve their writing and storytelling skills. In 2011, he founded Story Help Groups and joined the Roaring Writers ministry seven years later to encourage and equip all Christians to tell their life-changing stories. Besides writing his own books, Frank Ball does ghostwriting, copy editing, and graphic design to help others publish high-quality books. He coaches writers, writes blogs, and is a panelist on The Writer's View, an email discussion group.

He has taught at writer's conferences and churches across the U.S. and Canada. As Pastor of Biblical Research and Writing for three years, he wrote sermons, teaching materials, and hundreds of devotions.

His first book, *Eyewitness: The Life of Christ Told in One Story*, puts all the biblical information on the life of Christ into a chronological story that reads like a novel. *Born Blind: Voice of a Visionary* is a novel about the first-century blind Jew who was healed when he washed his eyes in the Siloam pool. *The Discussion Bible* has thousands of unanswered discussion questions to stir people's thoughts. *Storytelling at Its Best* is a practical guide for effective storytelling.

Career Years

Frank worked in the business world for forty years. Titles he has held are Salesman, Sales Manager, VP of Sales, Executive VP, Computer Programmer, Systems Analyst, VP of Information Systems, Purchasing Manager, Personnel Manager, and VP of Production. In all his years in business, he spent nights and weekends doing biblical research, teaching, preaching, and counseling. In 1996, he became a part-time writer seeking to tell the gospel story in a way that people who didn't read the Bible would know about Jesus. Ten years later, he became a full-time freelance writer, teacher, and speaker, encouraging people to discover their stories and learn to tell them well.

Growing Up:

Frank's birth certificate says he was born in 1945 in Manhattan, Kansas. At that time, a gallon of milk cost 62 cents, a loaf of bread was 19 cents, and gasoline was 16 cents per gallon. His family moved to the Houston area in 1954 and to Fort Worth in 1962. He was working part time at the age of twelve, and has held the following jobs. (1) Egg Salesman, (2) Janitor, (3) Elevator Operator, (4) Dish Washer, (5) Computer Programmer, (6) Warehouseman, (7) Welder, (8) Roofer, (9) Lawn Care Professional, (10) Leather Craftsman, (11) Personnel Manager, (12) Computer Hardware Technician, (13) **Auto Mechanic**, (14) Deliveryman, (15) Office Supply Salesman, (16) Freelance Writer, (17) Copy Editor, (18) Associate Pastor, (19) Public speaker, (20) Business Consultant, (21) Counselor, and (22) Carpenter. One item in the list was work without pay.

Frank is a widower since 2003, when his wife of thirty-seven years died of primary pulmonary hypertension. He has three married sons and seven grandchildren. He lives in an upstairs apartment, built in the huge attic of his oldest son's house in a Fort Worth suburb.

Books by the Author

Eyewitness: The Life of Christ Told in One Story

All the Bible's information about Jesus in a chrono-logical story that reads like a novel. Better than a harmony of the Gospels where we lack information from non-Gospel biblical text and have to mentally merge details from different Gospel accounts.

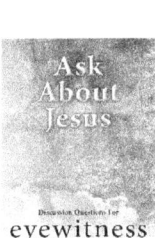

Ask About Jesus

A companion guide for use with *Eyewitness: The Life of Christ Told in One Story* for private meditation or group interactions. Thousands of thought-provoking questions can stir our passion to know the Lord better and bring us closer to him.

Eyewitness Inspiration: Contemporary Vignettes for Life

A collection of stories based on faith, fantasy, and fact that reveal the motives of historical figures as well as the passion of people as ordinary as your next door neighbors.

God's Plan

A six-week chronological study of the life of Christ covering the period from the beginning to Jesus at age twelve. In each session's stories, the storytelling style retains the biblical and historical information, yet gives you the kind of captivating experience you'd find in a bestselling novel.

The Discussion Bible

All sixty-six books of the Bible in easy-to-read verses. Thousands of questions encourage personal insight, open for people to freely speak their minds without fear of being wrong.

Born Blind: Voice of a Visionary

Cursed with blindness, Tuphlos had to keep asking, seeking, and knocking if he expected to become any better than a beggar. Then one day, he met a man who gave him sight and had a story to tell that should never be forgotten.

10 Thoughts to Ponder Series

A buffet for inquisitive minds. Each thought in these books are possible gems waiting to be polished. Discover the truth yourself by stirring your God-given reasoning power.

www.ingramcontent.com/pod-product-compliance
Lightning Source LLC
Chambersburg PA
CBHW070640050426
42451CB00008B/245